THE WISDOM OF AUTHENTICITY

YOUR SELF TO DISCOVER

STEPHEN K. SIMS

Published by Stephen K. Sims (Montreal, Canada)
First Edition, May, 2015.

Library and Archives Canada Cataloguing in Publication
Sims, Stephen, 1947-, author
The Wisdom of Authenticity: your self to discover

Issued in print and electronic formats.
ISBN 978-0-9940899-0-8 (paperback)
ISBN 978-0-9940899-1-5 (e-book)

1. Self-actualization (Psychology). I. Title.
BF637.S4S578 2015   158.1
C2015-902290-8
C2015-902291-6

Cover design: Drew MacEachern
Layout: Carole Zabbal-Wynne
Primary photographer: Dainius Juras

Parts of this publication may be reproduced and transmitted to anyone without the written permission of the author – for non-commercial uses only / excerpts to be shared for educational purposes, reflection and dialogue.

For quantity sales (discounts available), contact the author at steve@stephenksims.com.

Also published by author: *River of Awareness* (2009)
For further information, please visit www.stephenksims.com.

To all on the quest for authenticity
and a true path of meaning.

Contents

PROLOGUE

PART ONE: RIGHT INTENTION

1. Longing
2. Integral Potential
3. Dance of Change
4. The Anxious Ego
5. Path of Integrity

PART TWO: EMERGENT AWARENESS

6. Practice of Presence
7. Questions in Motion
8. Art of Discernment
9. Web of Error
10. Wisdom in Action

PART THREE: FIRE OF LOVE

11. Self-affirmation
12. Quantum Friendship
13. Interdependence
14. Peace Consciousness
15. Authentic Bliss

ACKNOWLEDGEMENTS

ABOUT THE AUTHOR

Prologue

The privilege of a lifetime is being who you are.
Joseph Campbell

I felt considerable stress during the time of my initiation into young adult identity, causing me to reflect seriously upon the purpose of my life and to question whether I was in *the right story* or not. This tension of inner alienation made me eager to find a sound direction of meaning. Little did I then know that my restless seeking would lead me on an adventure of self-discovery that would last a lifetime – a truly privileged journey, blessed with wonderful companions every step of the way.

In 1982, after a seven-year work involvement in a drug rehabilitation project in Montreal, I formed two dialogue circles among friends to explore themes related to the wisdom of personal transformation. The questions and insights we shared in our weekly exchanges over a nine-month period empowered each of us to give shape to the stories that our lives were asking us to write.

These conversations were the forerunners of numerous interactive learning circles across the planet – several thousand participants strong, over a 33-year span. The *search for authenticity* constituted the pulse of our relentless enquiry into the *wisdom of life*. This book creates a window into one such dialogue circle: 15 friends on a quest to identify personal purpose, vision and values.

The journey into authenticity draws us into a world of love that heals our darkest fears. It is a journey upon which we slowly discover our original potential and find genuine happiness. There is no arrival, no full achievement of authenticity – but as we withdraw from ways of inauthenticity, we come in touch with the reality of both our inner goodness and our outer giftedness.

The Wisdom of Authenticity has three main focuses: *right intention, emerging awareness*, and the *fire of love*. The way of attention gives one's journey to wholeness its energetic momentum, engendering a keen connection to our lived experience. Indeed, self-awareness is crucial, and develops from a quality of self-presence and self-understanding. It is directed towards the inner befriending of self and a deep communion with others.

True human potential finds expression in unlimited generosity, boundless ingenuity, and unconditional love. How do we best respond to the inner restlessness that resides in the tension between what is and what is yet to be? For each of us, an epic journey of learning and loving unfolds out of life's endless summons to transformation – the invitation to live more consciously, more creatively, more compassionately. Obedience to that summons brings us into the blissful experience of human authenticity.

1. Longing

*Before I can tell my life what I want to do with it, I must
listen to my life telling me who I am.*
Parker Palmer

*There is a certain way of being human that is my way. I am
called to live my life in this way, and not in imitation of
anyone else's. But this gives a new importance to being true
to myself. If I am not, I miss the point of my life…*
Charles Taylor

*…wholeness of personality is not a goal that is off in the
future; it is a condition of being that becomes present in the
course of the work that seeks it.*
Ira Progoff

inner fire

"My inner fire was out, totally out – I felt so lost!" recounted Scott at breakfast one morning, "Reality was hitting me hard. I had no motivation, no drive. I was nineteen years old, and in a real no man's land. I felt totally unprepared for changes that were taking place in my life." As Scott told his tale of mapping out young adult identity, I could hear the depth of the frustration and discouragement he had experienced.

"Doing drugs became a way of escape, though it certainly didn't help matters. I was making a lot of wrong choices. I was haunted by the fear of staying stuck in an inauthentic life. My life had a lot of potential that wasn't happening. I was longing for change, and definitely knew I needed to make some kind of a leap."

"As a kid I didn't question myself," Scott continued. "Only later on, I began to ask myself if what was going on in my life was real or not. When you are not being authentic,

Scott Simons

you feel very uncomfortable. You get really discouraged. I got to the point of feeling totally annoyed with myself."

"It was right when I was feeling most down on myself that I made the decision to get real." Scott's face lit up: "There is an aliveness you feel the second you leap into the air – even though you have no idea where your feet are going to land."

Scott's feet landed in the woods that summer when he was nineteen, and he lived ten drug-free weeks in deep nature. "This was a breakthrough experience that brought me back to who I was before I started using drugs. It brought back my Scott-ness. I felt fire inside me again!" He paused, before adding: "It was through this experience that I discovered my life purpose: to help people come back to health, and back to themselves."

Like Scott, even as we taste the annoyance of life not-being-lived, we hear inside ourselves a compelling call to authenticity. Often born out of discouragement or deep regret, sometimes dark desperation, inner aspiration surfaces to point us in the direction of the real life that awaits us. In the very mud of inauthenticity, once the imagination is stirred, an impassioned vision begins to germinate.

The drama of day-to-day living certainly seems to be characterized by an ever-present tension between authenticity and inauthenticity. This tension reveals the inner longing we all experience to become who we are beyond illusion and the strivings of the ego. This tension bids each of us to live the truth of our lives with openness and courage.

In modern jargon, we talk about *getting real*. Through attentiveness to the call to become deeply human, we allow ourselves to be guided by values and choices that put us on a path of authenticity. Through learning to open our hearts, we discover what it means to live a genuine life.

Human striving reflects a whole gamut of desire – from basic physical needs to the deeper longings of the heart. Certain drives focus on survival, sexual fulfillment, and the acquisition of power. On the spiritual level, we experience a thirst for self-knowledge and wisdom, and a strong yearning for love. In search of the essential self, our desires often pull us in different directions, and compete with one another. It then becomes necessary to sort out these different drives, and evaluate our choices in terms of their congruence with values that lead us to true freedom. If one finds and follows one's unique personal meaning, inner harmony is happily realized.

But, confined to a strictly materialistic domain, we live at the mercy of the ego and its wild ambitions disconnected from the higher purpose of our lives. Self-centred motivations try to make the *false self* true, but actually set us on a path of self-alienation. Boxed inside narrow notions of happiness, disillusionment is inevitable. For a time, we ride what seems to be a wave of success, but in the end experience emptiness born in a vacuum of meaning. As we learn to differentiate between the voices that pull us into self-deception and those that reveal the essential self, we are empowered to let go of ego-striving and surrender to higher purpose.

I was graced to face that challenge when, at the age of 22, I left Canada and set forth on a journey that would take me around the planet, but more importantly, led me into a new vision of being. It was then that I heard an inner voice speak: "Make your life an adventure of love". In that experience of awakening, new insights followed. I became more in touch with my core values, and realized that at the heart of my longing was the call to be a man for others.

The map I was making for my life changed from that point on, and a new path towards personal potential began to unfold. My outer journey, provoked by the deep unrest that I experienced as a young man, induced me to jump into an inner journey of self-discovery. Better attuned to the unconscious level inside myself, I was able to find a sound direction of meaning.

The longing for deep bliss that we meet inside ourselves ignites the quest to find personal fulfilment – it begs us to give ourselves permission to be who we are. To take possession of genuine happiness, each of us is invited to embrace our unique destiny. Thus, one's task of self-development lies in identifying our particular life purpose. Embarking on this journey as a young man, I dared myself to find and follow the path of meaning that was congruent with my true destiny – in this way, I began to taste the bliss of authenticity.

into the unknown

Over and over in one's lifetime, we are faced with making the choice between openness or contraction – either exploring the unknown or clinging to the familiar. If we stubbornly refuse the questions our lives ask of us, we stay in a shell of the known and repress self-discovery. Even then, a desire for authenticity haunts us and tries to provoke the awakening of our undiscovered selves.

Authenticity will certainly call us into a world of no-telling-what-is-possible, counteracting the common tendency to become embedded in beliefs that set limits on what is possible. With progressive self-knowledge, our rigid vision-constricting beliefs are unmasked, enabling us to expand our horizon of possibility.

To respond to the pull of authenticity is to put oneself in a position of openness – one must step into the unknown. Increasingly drawn by the power of wonder, new leaps of learning connect us to our hidden selves. Questions arise that guide us into a new vision of reality, and challenge us to remain open to the unexpected – to the surprise of who we are. The big question life asks each of us is: what am I here to do?

Out of fear, however, we often prefer *answers* to *questions*. Though we try to impose our will onto the future, in the end, we find ourselves at odds with our real meaning. But is it not true that any attempt to nail down the uncertain future turns out to be an exercise in futility? We cannot make the unknown known – the path ahead of us is both indefinite and infinite. Continuous self-enquiry helps one attain the right clues that point to the hidden self one does not yet know. Each individual's task is to draw forth our unique talent potential.

Because we cannot force the future, or manufacture visions, we watch and wait. New intentions emerge. And slowly each of us, in dialogue with the truths and values that are at the heart of our lives, awakens a path of purpose. Right direction links each of us to the creativity of the whole, empowering us to create a life in service of something larger than the private self.

interference

Scott identifies *ambivalence* as his greatest personal demon, one he has had to confront "too many times". Less discouraged than he used to be, Scott generalizes about learning to befriend doubt in a more creative way: "You feel a lot of ambivalence. It's part of the process you have to go through. You experience both authenticity and inauthenticity. You are confronted with having to make choices. You have to face the dissatisfaction you feel with the world you are in, and trust that what you don't like about your life will guide you to a life you do like."

"Doubting yourself is a hard place to be. You start second-guessing yourself. You get stuck in the middle. Sometimes you feel you are moving forwards, sometimes backwards. It is good, then, to ask yourself: is the next step in line with your intention, in line with your authenticity? As you listen to your doubt, your ambivalence slowly begins to dissolve. It brings you to a place of self-acceptance and self-love. Then you can go into the world with better confidence in yourself."

By asking myself the same question I had asked Scott about what it means to live a genuine life, I came to see a number of traps that held me back from actualizing my true self. In particular, I honed in on five different sources of interference: self-mistrust, envy, resentment, extreme busyness, and excessive idealism.

Learning to overcome *self-mistrust* and assert my own choices was a slow process that required steady growth in self-affirmation. Certainly the outside world sabotages our power of self-determination, and persuades us to live lives that are not our own. Perhaps the hardest part is getting unhooked from prescriptive parental agendas. We get swept along, in a similar vein, by strong social expectations, and live in accord with cultural programming that deeply conditions the limited way we see ourselves. To the extent that we allow ourselves to be defined from the outside in, more than from the inside out, we forfeit the authorship of our lives. For myself, all too often,

I paid a price for giving away my power, and going along with the crowd.

Another stumbling block was *envy*: dwelling on what I did not have, and wanting things to be the way they were not. It is easy to get caught up in the unreality of wishing for a life different from one's own. Everyone else appears to be better off: healthier, more successful, more easy-going, having more advantage and abundance. In the end, such striving amounts to self-torture, and is totally in vain. It was for me a form of self-abandonment that diverted attention from my real possibilities. So the questions I had to wrestle with were: how to come home to myself, how to find the courage to accept my fate with its particular burdens of darkness, how to truly live and love my own unique destiny. In truth, I had so much to be thankful for.

Akin to envy was *resentment*, whereby I would find myself in the powerlessness of the victim position. The true power of freedom is forfeited when we define our lives as effects of given conditions and conditioning rather than results of value-based choices. As long as we generate excuses and justifications, we get stuck in the stories we tell about why our lives are not working. I have never stayed very long in any victim narrative, but from time to time made visits to that territory of powerlessness. I knew when I was discounting my possibilities.

Extreme *busyness*, the pathology of modern culture, acted as another deterrent to authenticity. I had to learn that when I run around and get caught up in too much activity and endless distractions, self-intimacy is compromised. Without inwardness, gaps in self-awareness accrue, self-determination is short-circuited, and I become embedded in unconscious habits of thinking and feeling and acting. Certainly, whenever I do not take enough time for myself, I lose touch with who I am and start to run on empty.

A fifth trap for me was *misplaced idealism*. Born of ego strivings, I would push for perfection and demand of myself extreme achievement. Ego-based visions always get us into a lot of trouble – they tend to be lofty, and lend to excessive ambition, distorted expectations, and no end to frustration. Often I would chase after ill-fitting goals, and, as a consequence, experience extreme stress from aiming too high.

tending the fire

Scott's metaphor of inner fire symbolized for him the call of authenticity – the invitation to affirm what he would describe as "his real Scott-ness." I believe it is true that we each carry a certain measure of unconscious guilt inside ourselves with respect to our *unlived lives*. I know that when I listen to those inner tensions of not-feeling-right with myself, I am able to identify hidden aspects of the unrealized dream of my life.

When we first set forth on the journey of self-discovery, we have only a vague notion of where we are going and what we want, but progressively, step by step, the way is opened. Joseph Campbell urges us to "follow our bliss" and suggests that, over and above the sacrifices required, doors will always open. Beyond an initial vision, new questions continuously emerge to help clarify our life purpose, discern our deepest values, and refine our goals.

Scott knows well that the challenge of becoming-his-own-man is daunting, and he emphasizes the importance of "keeping the inner fire burning". And when asked how to do that, he responded: "It takes courage, and you have to find people to support you on your path of authenticity.

It's not that there is no fear – you have to go through the fear that is there, and that's the scary part."

As our breakfast drew to a close, Scott concluded: "Every day you have to remind yourself and commit yourself to inner work. You can't grasp authenticity once and for all. There is a practice involved. You have to keep adding logs to the fire. That fire helps you discover your true beauty. You feel a lot of enthusiasm. Tending the fire every single day brings joy – the fire becomes your best friend."

"Every day you have to remind yourself and commit yourself to inner work. You can't grasp authenticity once and for all. There is a practice involved."

2. Integral Potential

*Awakening brings its own assignments,
unique to each of us … you are a seed, a silent promise.*
Marilyn Ferguson

It often happens that the potentialities in the individual do not wait silently for their opportunity to emerge but that they press, strain, clamor, disturb the entire personality until an avenue of expression is opened for them.
Ira Progoff

*We are creatures of excellence and intelligence and skill.
We can be free. We can learn to fly.*
Richard Bach

the big secret

Most of the time, Christelle radiates an upbeat anything-is-possible energy, and I was curious to find out how she sources and sustains her optimism. Christelle was willing to let me in on her big secret: "From an early age my mother motivated me to be the best that I could be, insisting that I place my standards high and reminding me that I was granted opportunities she, as a child, could only dream of. Growing up, I wanted her to be proud of what I accomplished. I felt it was my responsibility to be successful because I was given the chance."

"It's very interesting, as I look back, to remember that I always had a deep core belief that I could be anything I wanted to be. It sounded crazy to a lot of my friends when I would speak about achieving great things. I didn't know what, I didn't know how, but I knew it would happen. I could sense that so many people were stuck in their unhappiness, and there was no way I wanted that to be me."

Christelle Francois

"This achieving great success was like a big secret that I had with myself. I wouldn't disclose too many of my dreams in fear that other people's doubts would affect my confidence in realizing them. It is not that I felt chosen, or better than others, but I kept more to myself knowing that many individuals don't buy the idea that everyone has the potential to be great and that everyone has a unique purpose. My mom was wonderful for she always instilled a great confidence in my dreams."

I questioned Christelle about the danger of self-inflation, and whether there was a dark side to aiming so high. She was candid in her response: "I have crash-landed, I have fallen, I have been disappointed, I have felt ashamed," as she described her experience of setbacks and failures. "But every time I have negative experiences or go through failure, I eventually get into a zone of acceptance – what's happening is just part of the ride. I don't like to stay in my misery too long. I pray hard during the low times, and am able to recover my peace."

Christelle continued: "I have made some big mistakes that have cost me, especially when my ego was trying to run the show. In my difficult moments, I have learned how to better take care of myself. I see obstacles as another chapter in a bigger story. I have learned to keep a positive perspective, to keep moving forward, and to focus on what I like doing, on the things I really feel passionate about. That way, I can re-awaken my confidence and get back on my bliss track."

"By keeping a focus on your innate talents, you help the process move forward. When you match your natural gifts with a rigorous work ethic, you have an explosive combination. Everyone, if they work at it, has the potential to be successful and live a life of happiness. It is your birthright."

seeds of authenticity

A seed holds a silent promise – the possibility of what it can become when fully matured. Its power to grow is generated from within, but, of course, it must be planted in an environment that enables its growth. The image of a seed, I think, serves as an apt metaphor to describe the emergence of human potential. Seeds have an eagerness to grow, and bear fruit. Each contains a direction of development, and draws forth its maturation through a sequence of transformations. Over time, as a seed releases its latent potential, it reveals fields of possibility not previously evident.

Likewise, the future lies hidden inside ourselves. Similar to a seed, the gift that one's life represents awaits maturation and manifestation. The principle of growth expresses itself in a thrust towards the realization of the true self. We are moved towards something greater, and in order to discover our higher possibilities, it is necessary to push beyond routine expectations of self. Only as we come into contact with the essence of who we are, are we able to refine our understanding of what it means to live a genuine life.

Inner intelligence lies at the heart of human authenticity, ever pushing us in the direction of integral growth. We are internally organized towards a specific purpose, and each individual has a unique story that awaits expression. As we bring forth our special gifts in response to our deepest longings, each of us creates a singular path. True intention and true talent find each other, and develop together.

Everything we interact with is setting up a trajectory of development, or decline. From day to day, we choose different environments to live in, and to a large measure the fruit we bear is a function of where we are planted. Optimal growth requires a soil that is fertile, together with the right amount of sunshine and water.

The way to cultivate a garden is to coax its growth. So too, seeds of authenticity that contain our creative capacities require gentle, steady nurture. There are tremendous potentialities to be awakened and developed. With the right type of coaxing, human growth is guided towards full flourishing. Otherwise, in conditions that are inhospitable, like when soil or rain is deficient, or sunshine lacking, development is arrested.

Christelle sings her mother's praise with respect to the encouragement she received from her: "When I think of potential, I think of a seed which will bloom if it is fed. You will not achieve your potential by being pushed to perform – the realization of potential is an organic growth process, more pure than a performance-driven dynamic. What helped me was my mom's style of pushing me. When I failed, she would still be very supportive and encourage me to go on. My mom gave me permission to fail – I would cry and she would say it's okay. She didn't only love me when I did well."

Seeds of authenticity readily germinate when we enter a world of love. Beyond our needs for physical survival and psychic fulfilment, we can make a leap into a bigger story of meaning. Our deep longing for freedom points towards pure possibility where, in the experience of love, we are brought into a connection with the whole of life.

As potentiality begins to emerge, we find ourselves in a garden that is alive with growth. In the interface of our differentiated life stories, we come to recognize that we belong to one big interconnected story – the beauty of the garden manifests in the mix of our individual achievements of self-actualization.

burdens of darkness

There is, I think, a fine line between potential and limitation, between power and powerlessness. All of us struggle with difficult trials, and sometimes suffer bitter defeats. Indeed, the force of circumstances bears down on our lives in different ways, and each of us is required to carry a particular burden of darkness. Though the myth of limitless potential suggests that we can overcome all obstacles, feelings of impotence exist as a very real counter-position to our dreams of utopian omnipotence. In truth, life has its harsh limits.

To some extent, an individual's burdens define a horizon of possibilities. There are persons who live with serious physical handicaps, others who have experienced deep emotional trauma. Some individuals have been devalued, shamed, and deeply wounded in their self-esteem. There are also those who have been victims of injustice, and have lived in historical contexts of war and hunger and abject poverty. And all too often, we hear stories of physical and psychological abuse that speak of unimaginable violence.

Further obstacles to freedom include the burden of our own ethical failures, ego blunders, and entrenchment in self-defeating behaviours. All of us experience human frailty, exhaustion, and weakness. Our personal development can also be thwarted by spiritual inertia, and by misguided choices that accrue from inattentiveness, ignorance, and short-sighted self-interest.

But even as we come face-to-face with lack and limitation, with human imperfection and sorrow, with helplessness and hopelessness, the human spirit rises to confront the force of darkness invoking the light and love that dissolve its power. And even though our lives seem to sometimes be as much defined by our disabilities as by our abilities, we must confront our habits of downplaying possibility and escaping into despair. Do we too readily deny our talents, and buy into defeat?

The tall challenge from inside any prison of inner or outer darkness is to affirm what is truly possible even as we acknowledge our reduced possibilities. Humility embraces and accepts real limitations, but does not argue for them – it sets us free from the frustration of trying to achieve beyond our reach of talent. In spite of fate, which imposes certain parameters on individual potential, the challenge for anyone is to move beyond cramped intentions into an open-ended exploration of purpose and possibility.

In one way or another, life is always urging us to dare our dreams. Beyond injury and entrapment and victimization, beyond all the constrictions of past and present, there is a freedom that is won when we avoid locking personal identity into a notion that is defined by powerlessness. It is important to know the difference between a misplaced idealism that produces ill-fitting goals and a well-grounded, optimistic realism that bids us search for the higher consciousness that breaks through despair. Ironically, is it not the tragic aspects of human experience that summon us to new horizons of hope?

imagining possibility

Though sometimes characterized as an idealist, I never apologize for chasing perfection and believing in the unimaginable. Indeed we live on a planet that is anything but ideal, but what motivates the task of history (and my life) is the dream of a better world.

Otherwise, one's outlook becomes jaded and we readily succumb to the temptation of cynicism and despair. When we feel that 'what is' is all there is, life has nowhere to go – then there is no future, no story to create.

Inauthenticity talks a language of impossibility. When we concede hope, we give in to helplessness, and thereby refuse to believe in the possibility of realizing greater freedom and happiness. On the other hand, when love is activated, we release an abundance of imagination, intelligence, and innovation that builds a momentum of transformation. Our deeds of love aim to alleviate suffering, and bring as much joy as we can to a sorrowful world. Though the world cannot be made perfect, no doubt each of us can make a difference – a very big one!

The call to human potential commands both fear and fascination. The Latin word for power is *potens* from which is derived the word *potential*. As dormant powers inside ourselves wait to be awakened, we sense that there is an exciting quest at hand. At the same time, we feel terrified of the unknown. Yet the summons is persistent, and despite some inner resistance, we are beckoned to open ourselves up to a destiny that draws forth our deepest capacity for love.

When the journey that connects us to our personal power is initiated, often a powerful symbol or metaphor will appear – an image that captures our mind and heart, that releases vitality and points the way towards one's authentic path. Images arise from different stratums of the unconscious – from dreams, buried emotions, and deep inner intelligence. Such images serve to create powerful metaphors of meaning, and as we sift through the images that arise, we come in touch with our deepest values.

By nourishing imagination, we move closer to our true essence, and progressively are able to affirm our boundless possibilities. The products of the imagination guide the development of consciousness, and draw forth an inner truth that finds expression in language and conceptual thought. Beyond our previous imagining, symbols open up new paths into our future.

It is necessary to follow this inward process of growth until potentialities latent in the unconscious become manifest. Tapping into the inexhaustible energies of life, the intelligence of the universe that dwells inside us allows us to take possession of greater freedom and happiness. The more we listen to the summons of the infinite, we find clues that reveal new directions of artistic expression, scientific enquiry, athletic achievement, intellectual curiosity, and spiritual creativity.

As we awaken purpose, we activate potential, and overcome the helplessness we feel in front of external reality, thereby undoing some of our disabling anxieties. Self-affirmation sets a journey of freedom in motion, and self-awareness gives that journey its momentum. Our personal power is actualized through cultivating a sustainable practice of authenticity – self-presence, insight and discernment, and actions based on right intention. Self-knowledge enables us to discover more and more of ourselves, and appropriate ever greater authenticity.

The triumph of potential is hard-won, or as Christelle puts it: "To find your inner truth, you have to become vulnerable, and really open yourself up to yourself. When you listen to yourself, you come into a place of self-knowledge. You feel right with yourself when you are truthful with yourself. As fear is eliminated, you get closer to your inner truth."

"When you match your natural gifts with a rigorous work ethic, you have an explosive combination. Everyone, if they work at it, has the potential to be successful and live a life of happiness. It is your birthright."

3. Dance of Change

The snake that cannot shed its skin must perish.
Friedrich Nietzsche

*And the courage to be as oneself
is the courage to make of oneself
what one wants to be.*
Paul Tillich

*Especially we fear becoming someone we do not as yet know.
To liberate the desire for this becoming is to come into the
perfect love that casts out fear.*
Sebastian Moore

living non-stop

"Even when I recognized that I needed to change, I didn't act out of what I knew. There were forces inside me putting up resistance – it really is so hard to change! How long does it take to truly realize that we are going in the wrong direction?"

Eli's life is in high gear most of the time – combining motherhood with a challenging professional career and a fast-paced lifestyle. But she has been reflecting a lot of late about changing the dance she is in. "I was wanting too much," Eli continued. "I was living with an image of myself that demanded continuous high performance. I needed to be perfect. The expectations I placed on myself left me feeling disappointed, angry, and sad."

"Finally I reached a tipping point: insomnia with high irritability, and I had a small breakdown in my body. I was going way too fast – my body was telling me to slow down. I could not meet the high standards I had set for myself, and was totally unable to relax. My suffering was extreme – mostly, I was really scared of losing control. My head was spinning and spinning. I had pushed myself one time too many."

Eli Perreau-Linck

"This was the turning point," Eli continued, and her voice began to convey a tone of serenity. "I finally committed to change. I just started walking more slowly, and I felt better right away. When I slow down, everything becomes much clearer. I have more awareness. It is not just a question of slowing down, but of changing my perspective on what I really want, where I am going, and where I need to be right now."

Eli reflected back on the pressures she had felt from the outside world, and "how hard it is to just be yourself." But at this point in time, she was clear that she needed to unbind herself from an over-ambitious anxiety-driven agenda, and reclaim more of her true self. It was time to choose the change that her life was insisting upon.

"The real breakthrough came when I said to myself, 'I have to stop!' I made three decisions and took action immediately. I felt a burst of new inner energy. In that decisive moment, I took part in the change I had to live."

growth edges

If one is to find a genuine path, it is necessary to experience life in terms of change and development. Regardless of how life meets us, or we meet it, we are carried along on a fast-moving tide into the mysterious unknown and thrown into a never-ending adventure of self-discovery. Attentiveness to the process along with conscious intention set us forth on the quest for authenticity – seeking out a world of wisdom and love, there to find true bliss.

The human life cycle is a non-stop event – the one thing we know is that our lives never stand still.

At every turn, life insists on newness, and takes us to our growth edges where predictability and security constantly must be relinquished. Personal identity evolves through the different passages of time, and has to undergo redefinition again and again.

As Eli learned, during the destabilization that comes with any life transition, finding the right pace for oneself is essential. Change brings with it different degrees of risk and stress – both need to be skilfully managed. In meeting the unknown, we are required to hold a delicate tension between protection and vulnerability. Even as we open ourselves to new possibility, a measure of stability needs to be secured: one foot grounded in the known, as the other negotiates the not-yet-known.

Each of us develops at a different pace – the force of circumstances, the degree of support, one's temperament and psychological disposition, the cultural context, and one's overall readiness for change are all variables that come into play. Managing change well entails learning how to carry the tension that change requires, while avoiding harmful levels of distress. In times of deep discouragement, or times when one is feeling overwhelmed, it is essential to set aside some down time to honour one's need for rest and rejuvenation.

A good question to ask is: how do we identify and move to our growth edge, and stay there, without actually going over the edge? Risk and recklessness are not the same. Prudent risk discerns danger, and dares an appropriate level of uncertainty. It paces change. On the other hand, recklessness involves uncalculated risk – it is a form of bravado, an ego-driven leap into the unknown. Recklessness pushes too fast, and refuses to take the time to differentiate between smart and foolish risk.

Reluctance to change reveals itself when we attempt to stay in a world that no longer exists, and thus protect an *unreality*. Clinging to the known is a root cause of stress – certainly, any excessive attachment to the past or present brings inevitable suffering. Hanging on to the status quo feeds a resistance to growth that intensifies our darkness, and lies at the heart of inauthenticity.

The danger of the dark unknown always triggers plenty of adrenaline, and often we feel at the mercy of forces of fate that render us powerless. So we hold back from the task of transformation. We opt to stay in our comfort zone, and settle for dull mediocrity.

This inability to trust new possibility blocks the bringing forth of our latent potential. In this way, the ego wins out and deafens us to the call to embrace the task of authenticity.

In fact, the ego does everything it can to protect its own agenda – it defends its blind spots and resists the enlargement of consciousness. To whatever extent one is trapped in the narrow world of the ego, one's existence becomes framed by security and power needs. Thereby, one forgoes the wide-open adventure of self-discovery that draws us into richer experiences of meaning. Sooner or later, though, the law of change will require a meltdown of the ego even as it tenaciously tries to hold its pose.

beginning again

The dawning of each year evokes a certain pitch of excitement that speaks to the never-ending drama of authenticity and inauthenticity playing out in our lives. There is regret and new resolve, gratitude and hope, often a heightened appreciation of meaningful relationships. Inevitably it seems, as the calendar turns, a strong desire for change surfaces – we want to play for higher stakes, we want to begin again.

Likewise, at the different thresholds of change in our lives, authenticity makes a plea for greater attention – calling us to *get real*, to move beyond indifference, to keep curiosity alive, to learn thoroughly and live passionately. In the gaps between changes, the voice of human aspiration is perhaps heard the loudest. Certainly, whenever there is a sense of time running out, we feel a greater urgency to refine self-awareness, clarify values, make new choices, and act more decisively.

The exercise of re-focusing intention gives evidence of a determination to go on growing. Motivation for change, too, is born out of inner emptiness and different varieties of discontent. We long to transform the human desperation arising in conditions of poverty, injustice, lack and limitation, hypocrisy, confusion, ignorance, fear, grief, betrayal, and loneliness. In each of us abides a yearning to be set free from these burdens of darkness.

All of us have known moments when we have felt totally helpless, or periods in our lives when we have lost our way. At its worst, such helplessness can slide into hopelessness. Each time we hit a wall – anxiety, meaninglessness, loss of motivation, moral decline, inner conflicts, relationship breakdown, physical illness – we keenly experience our human vulnerability.

Yet hope springs anew in the very midst of human desperation. We hear it said, darkest before the dawn – sometimes, quite suddenly, light breaks into our nighttime, and difficult trials give way to a new day. Such was Eli's experience when she made a decisive choice for greater authenticity.

One's attitude towards change largely defines one's relationship to hope. Hope is born out of knowing that we need to change, accepting as true that we really can change, and choosing to move beyond our comfort zones. Hope believes in greater possibilities, and is ready to risk the unknown. It is ready to dare the discovery of reality.

All too commonly, however, we buy into cynicism or despair, and allow ourselves to become entrenched in the same thought patterns for years, if not for a lifetime. Or, we cling to our emotional routines, to certain self-images, and to the stories we tell about ourselves in order to justify our personal dysfunction. Well-practiced at arguing for our limitations, we end up feeling powerless to change. Here Albert Einstein comes to mind – he describes the self-delusion that comes from doing the same things over and over, yet expecting different results.

A transformative process asks us to rise above timidity, to be ready to risk, to strain forwards. What must be refused is the temptation to become closed, to shut down possibility, to choose complacency. Change is about facing difficult trials and tests. It is about honesty, and cultivating rigorous self-knowledge. It is about making hard choices and letting go of secure routines. Change requires the determination to be conscious. Each threshold of change demands a letting go – like Eli, we are required to put certain elements of our lives behind us in order to move forwards.

Being open to revision asks for no small amount of courage. Courage is taking heart – and taking a leap when it is time to let go. How do we cultivate an openness that gives us access to the mystery of our own unfolding, even as we face into the radical uncertainty of the future? How do we confront our stubborn attachments to the status quo? How do we learn to become comfortable with the discomfort of change?

continuous emergence

My life work in awareness education has focused on supporting individuals through major life transitions – mapping adolescent growth, shaping young adult identity, negotiating the waters of mid-life, accompanying the terminally ill. The way forward always builds on an enlargement of understanding the development that is (or needs to be) happening, identifying resistances to change, and cultivating the readiness to go on growing.

Change is never easy. In fact, it is often quite messy, involving a lot of disorder and chaos. Self-discovery creates discontinuity – our habitual patterns of thinking, feeling, and acting must be set aside if we are to realize our true possibilities. This re-patterning happens on all levels: physical, mental, emotional, and spiritual.

In fact, everything in the world of form is subject to transformation. Our thought patterns and emotional habits are in continuous evolution and wear out in the play of time, as do our bodies. So too, personal identity is only provisional, and images of self undergo steady revision. Beyond form lies the mystery of who we are. As we befriend the complex dynamics of change, we become acquainted with the law of impermanence and learn to trust more deeply our emergence into new life.

Conscious transformation builds upon the determination to grow, and upon the surrender of inauthentic living in order to realize one's undiscovered self. Sustainable personal development results from the sum of many small changes oriented towards limitless potential. As we explore new dimensions of self, we allow our uniqueness to emerge. The cornerstone of authenticity is thorough self-knowledge.

There is an aphorism that says we do not grow old, rather we become old when we stop growing. To be *young* is to have a radical openness that allows the story of our lives to keep expanding. Indeed, constant growth is the real evidence of being truly alive. By discarding rigid self-definitions, we make room for new maps of meaning. Every threshold of change involves the death of an old self, and the emergence of greater possibility.

As we navigate the unknown, from becoming to becoming, uncertainty is our constant companion. We grow from disequilibrium. More and more in touch with the unconscious, we meet surprise. Learning to trust that something new is ready to come into our lives at each moment opens us up to the experience of breakthrough and the enjoyment of continuous rejuvenation.

The biggest lesson I have learned about change is that personal transformation is not about getting into a power struggle with ourselves. It is not about self-conquest, but about self-discovery. It involves willpower and courage, together with an abundance of self-awareness and wisdom. A ready-willing-aware self dances above the forces of fate and wins greater personal freedom. Empowered by steady intention, we truly become the dancers creating the change that ushers in deeper authenticity.

Eli's experience of being upended provoked her to create the next version of herself. Over time, she realized that getting out of a rut was ultimately about hearing and obeying the voice of her true self. And when our conversation ended, Eli had one last insight to share: "I have come to appreciate that the real agency for change resides right inside myself – I have to let the voice of authenticity within lead the way, and be willing to change. This releases a power of self-determination that works hand in hand with my growth in self-awareness."

"When I slow down, everything becomes much clearer. I have more awareness. It is not just a question of slowing down, but of changing my perspective on what I really want, where I am going, and where I need to be right now."

4. THE ANXIOUS EGO

The ego must die a thousand times before the self is born, and each little death is a rite of passage into larger life.
Sam Keen

The true self grows in inverse proportion to the growth of egoism.
Teilhard de Chardin

So long as we remain within the ego, we see the world only through the screen of our fears, our vanity, and our desire.
Oscar Ichazo

high on illusion

The only time I get to talk to Fabien these days is when he is stuck in rush hour traffic – this is his allotment of solitude between exhausting professional responsibilities and the endless demands of family life. One such telephone chat centered on *ego*, and Fabien, who likes to jump into a conversation with both feet, began with a terse declaration: "I'm still deep into ego!" He paused for a moment, and then added, "I never feel I am doing enough, and what I am doing is never good enough."

This was a big conversation opener, and I was curious to know, and asked him, what *not enough* was all about. "My childhood was all about not being good enough. I was always pushed to accomplish more. I was told I didn't amount to anything. I put a lot of energy into winning parental approval, and to this day I am always trying to prove myself – prove that I can do more than what others think I can do."

"My early adolescence was completely ego-driven. It was all about looking good, women, pleasure, being the best-dressed at parties, excelling as a drug user, having lots of money and a car. This is how I tried to build identity. It was my way of saying: hey, I am a somebody! It was all an illusion but, I guess, a necessary part of my growth."

Fabien Bergeron

The afternoon commuter traffic remained gridlocked – being stuck in traffic seemed an apt metaphor as Fabien went on to describe his "stuckness" in what seemed like an always-the-same emotional prison: "Even now I still feel the pressure to perform. It is constant! Perhaps unconsciously self-imposed. I am always trying so hard to impress others, as well as myself. I really need to free myself from this entrapment that is the result of wounding experiences in early childhood."

Fabien indicated that once in a while he feels a bit of short-lived relief from "…experiences of inner peace that help me realize that I don't have to prove myself or impress others. Unfortunately, these moments of calmness disappear all too soon, and my equilibrium gets derailed. Just when I think I'm cured, I lose focus on the processes that generated my serenity, and quickly find myself back in anxiety mode. That is when I get really discouraged and look for false gratifications."

At this point in our conversation, Fabien abruptly exclaimed: "Right now, it has just hit me: I gotta change fast! I think it all comes down to self-acceptance – learning to accept my limitations. I need to take action – I need to grow in self-awareness, spend more quiet time with myself, and pay attention to my physical wellness."

I asked Fabien if guilt came into the picture. "Man, guilt! I just have to look at my body – all the fatigue and wear-and-tear and unrelieved stress. I am not in the present moment. I'm always worrying about tomorrow, and as a salesman, always worrying about generating future sales. I feel guilty about not living my real life. I am forgetting about my real values. "

"It seems crazy," Fabien concluded, "but I think I have more to learn from my three-year-old son than to teach him. We spend time in the park together. I watch how he manages his needs and energy, and he knows how to have fun. He reflects different images of freedom that point to how I need to change. The only way for me to find serenity is to get back to my authentic self, somehow."

an empty fiction

The word *ego* has many different definitions with mostly negative connotations. Generally, it is described as only a small part of the total person, which keeps its attention on sustenance, self-protection, and social status. Throughout Fabien's self-narrative, we hear undercurrents of anxiety – we see how his need for approval is pushing him around, if not, running his life.

In early maturation, a sense of who we are emerges as we begin to come into the conscious recognition of our needs for physical nurture, emotional well-being, and social belonging. To the extent that one receives strong acceptance and affirmation, and feels safe in the world, one thrives in the pursuit of self-reliance. As one grows into the confidence of personal power through a wholesome adaptation to social reality, healthy ego develops.

Many individuals, however, live with deeply-wounded egos. Those who lack love, often the result of parental rejection or abandonment, will sometimes experience quite debilitating insecurity. Without steady physical and emotional nurture, personal growth is arrested and, needless to say, the ego forms in a very unhealthy manner. Such alienation is marked by damaged self-esteem, a lack of belonging, patterns of negative emotion, and maladaptive behaviors.

Over-identification with one's ego, healthy or wounded, puts one out of touch with one's true self. If an individual is unable to awaken genuine meaning and value, the ego builds its own fiction – it compensates by creating narratives of exaggerated self-importance, or of self-rejection. Both leave one feeling empty. Self-importance argues for being special – I am better than others. It craves power as a defense against weakness. Conversely, self-rejection takes up the victim position and argues for powerlessness – I am not okay. One draws attention to self by dramatizing one's wounds.

To be enclosed in an ego-bound world is to be locked into a small story about oneself without reference to a larger story of meaning and value. To one extent or another, the anxious ego hinders the development of our capacity for greater creativity and love. Only as we become aware of the ego's limited place within a bigger story of human meaning do we discover the whole person. Beyond performance and pretence, the essential self emerges and trumps the ego.

ego inflation

Usually, I equate the word *egoism* with ego inflation. Modern culture tends to live in the habitation of the inflated ego: conquest, achievement, identity based on privilege, image-making, competition, status-seeking, survival of the fittest, consumption, social reputation, spiritual pride. If we remain unschooled in the poetry of true happiness, we are truly prisoners of egotistic striving.

The ego by itself is ultimately impotent, exhausted in its limit of meaning. Much darkness accrues from behaviors that are rooted in the empty experience of one's own self-centered motivations. At the mercy of our anxieties and raw desires, genuine need turns to desperation and greed – revealed in our addictive grasping for money, food, drugs, sex, and transitory pleasure.

An inflated ego can be described as an unstable state of consciousness that struggles endlessly for its own survival. Steeped in narcissistic motivations, egoism focuses exclusively on self-protection – in a world of anxious striving, it pursues pleasure and profit, and feeds its own power drive. The ego, living in the dread of vulnerability, has an inordinate lust for control. Its game is bullying – anger arises when the ego cannot have its way, that is, when it meets the limits of its ability to control external reality.

Hand in hand with anger, arrogance takes root as the ego exaggerates its power in the lie of knowing-it-all. Or, when we take excessive pride in our achievement of virtue and talent, we fuel the inflation of the false self and build false pride.

The prolific author and philosopher Gerald Heard describes egoism in terms of the love of gain, pleasure, and fame, which in turn lead to possessiveness, addiction, and pretentiousness. The ego fears the loss of what is gained, dreads weakness and pain, and is afraid of lack and shame. His threefold antidote to egoism is: modesty (there is no lack), restraint (pleasure is fleeting), and anonymity (there is no one to impress).

Ego, for sure, likes to go it alone – it thinks of itself as separate, and lives in a narrow world of its own. Adept at rationalizing selfish motivations, the striving of the ego blinds us from the experience of authentic friendship. Indeed, when we are seduced by false desires, we find ourselves more and more alienated from others.

Wisdom through the ages has taught that when we choose to live for self and not for others, we are looking for happiness in the wrong place. Adding to this, the narcissistic ego hides the totality of who we are – whenever individual identity is defined in terms of the ego-personality, we mask the real self. Caught up in fear and ignorance, greed and grasping, we feed the illusion of the separate self.

But even as the ego flexes its muscle, every assertion of the false self in time runs out of steam – ego-bound ambition has nowhere to go. Inevitably frustration and fatigue arise when we become locked inside prisons of self-concern. To say the least, the futile strivings of the ego are doomed to fail –

symptoms of depression, isolation, addiction, violence, anxiety, anger, and despair inevitably arise, often in the extreme.

new freedom

The narrow ego ultimately needs to give way to the open heart. Beyond the many superficial motivations of ego consciousness, lie the miracle and mystery of authentic being. Though a prisoner of his need for validation, Fabien, all the while, longs to escape the entrapment of his anxious ego, and taste new freedom. His deep desire for authenticity is clearly mirrored back to him by his three-year-old son – the desire to get to the other side of anxiety and embrace his deeper self.

When we are ready to come to terms with our alienation, from both self and others, behaviors growing out of excessive ego identification become unmasked. This entails the willingness to let go of a false sense of control, and to surrender personal comfort to meet the challenges of change. By coming to know the ego as a narrow field of possibility, we open ourselves to a world of unimagined potential, and then begin to find our true place under the sun.

The tyranny of the ego consists in its insistence on independence – it denies the reality of interdependence. Because the ego resists truth, it is necessary to expose the lies the ego tells. Spiritual author Eckhart Tolle suggests that we cannot use the ego to fight the ego – we only end up with more egoism. The goal is not to conquer the ego, but to realize a world bigger than it. We do so by standing in front of self-deception with the truth of love.

The stronger the assertion of the ego, the larger the spiritual vision one needs to counteract its forcefulness. Gerald Heard suggests: a consciousness as much plus as it is minus is needed to reach the alienation that ensues when in the grip of the ego. It is when we open ourselves up to a new vision of reality and connect to a world of love that real change begins to happen.

Accordingly, the ego is not destroyed, but transcended. It loses its power when, through self-knowledge, we reference our lives to authentic meaning, and thereby come in touch with our intrinsic goodness – we learn to value our true selves. Any experience of transformation is built upon the expanding recognition and trust of our intrinsic goodness. As we identify a self bigger than ego, we create a life that is more and more real.

This comes about when ego identity yields to a higher intelligence and a larger love, and the false self surrenders to the authority of the true self. New consciousness transcends the illusion of separateness, and we realize that we are woven into an inclusive whole. Then we clearly see that personal fulfilment is based on the notion of a self that is integrally involved with the lives of others. We become fully alive through experiences of deep communion with those outside ourselves.

The transformation of identity all boils down to the awakening of one's journey towards wholeness, which gives birth to integrity, meaning, oneness, harmony, inclusion, and service to others. It is in the tension between ego and authenticity that the quest for the whole self is born – the call to transformation sets out a path of new intention that frustrates the assertions of the limited ego. The ego is reminded of its smallness, its ultimate impotence.

Something inside of us knows that outside the confinement of egoism lies the freedom that brings us into an experience of joy. As we enter into the real world of love, we taste aliveness as never before. The vision of one's authentic self empowers us to meet the ego and unmask its many illusions.

Fabien readily acknowledges being grid-locked inside an anxious ego. Finding himself caught up in the traffic of social images and survival anxieties, he feels himself entrapped in a performance-driven drama at the expense of living a more genuine life. A need for approval lies at the heart of his wounded ego. This has been played out in relationship first with his parents, then his peers, and now in the workplace.

All of us, like Fabien, are players in the theatre of the ego, struggling to find a way out of our fears, yet often frustrated by a sense of chronic imprisonment within a chaos of inauthenticity. How do we get beyond the small story of who we are and discover our true greatness?

As Fabien explores his anxiety drives, his evolving awareness is instrumental in helping him unlock ego patterns that will open the way for the serenity of his true self. His own words attest to his deep desire to be set free: "Right now, the bar is set low on authenticity, and high on illusion. Once I stop resisting change, I can take actions to make change happen. I have to get out of the discomfort I am used to, and risk the unknown. My goal is to create a sustainable serenity."

"I think I have more to learn from my three-year-old son than to teach him. We spend time in the park together. I watch how he manages his needs and energy, and he knows how to have fun. He reflects different images of freedom that point to how I need to change."

5. Path of Integrity

*There is no favourable wind for someone
who does not know where they are going.*
Seneca

*Instead of widespread satisfaction, we see the frenzies of
popular culture, the distractions of the idle, the rage of the
dispossessed, and only a rare person who moves through this
life with a sense of transcendent purpose, deep psychic
grounding, and a spiritually enlarged life.*
James Hollis

*Tension, a lack of honesty, and a sense of unreality
come from following the wrong force in your life.*
Joseph Campbell

true to self

When Lucas and I met for lunch, I suggested we throw around some thoughts on the theme of *integrity*. I have found that one way to initiate a lively conversation is to question the meaning of *integrity* – this word tends to elicit, in the interplay of self-expression, an extremely wide variety of reflections. I was feeling rather hungry, so I said to Lucas, "You do the talking, and you can leave the eating to me!"

Lucas Tomalty

My lunch mate seized the lead question (what does *integrity* mean in your own experience?) and ran with it: "Integrity is standing by your values, finding strength in your convictions, not giving into social pressures, being true to yourself. It is when you are firing on all cylinders, when everything is moving well together." He paused, and then went on to say: "Nobody can make you act with integrity. When you are faced with tough decisions, ultimately, it's you that makes the call – you are responsible for the choices you make."

Then, drifting in a new direction, Lucas put the focus on conflict resolution and truthful confrontation. "I spent a good part of my life trying to avoid conflict and confrontation. That avoidance of conflict brought on a lot of anxiety, and I internalized a lot of stress. Slowly I have been finding my voice, and learning to stand up for myself in circumstances where before I would be silent. With more self-confidence, I can now address issues head on, call others to task, and put forth my position based on values I choose for myself."

As the conversation continued to gather steam, there was no letting up in Lucas' flow of thoughts. "Integrity is wisdom. Acting with integrity is embracing the ideals that you are striving towards. Real wisdom includes action, not just knowledge. I get frustrated when my actions go against my values, when I act without virtue." I asked Lucas how he deals with that inner frustration when his actions contradict his values. "I try to remember what is most important, to get back to the awareness game, and to recognize when I am falling into any negative patterns. The more I practice awareness, the sooner I catch myself when I am off my game."

Lucas took another bite from his multi-layered sandwich, and then continued: "There is a lot of anxiety in the air these days. We have too many distractions. Social media and technology are making our lives more complicated. There is so much pressure to keep up financially. When I am a stress-case, the best remedy I know is awareness. It begins with being able to identify where my anxiety is coming from."

Here, the word *balance* came to mind for him. "I think a lot about balance which is another way of talking about integrity. To me, being off-balance is about losing focus, reacting rather than acting, and getting caught up in the daily melodrama of life. That's when I need to simplify my life, bring it down to the basics, and focus on what is most important to me. That's when I remind myself to eat and sleep well, take care of my body, and also pay quality attention to my relationships."

I invited Lucas to catch his breath before telling me a story or two related to choices that had helped strengthen his integrity. "One of my early tests involved coming to terms with peer pressure. Gradually I became aware that I was surrounded by quite a number of individuals in different parts of my life who were having a negative influence on me, who were bringing out the worst in me. I couldn't act according to my own values, and be true to myself. I came to realize that my personal integrity was being compromised, and furthermore, that popularity was not the most important thing in the world."

"Then one day, it just kind of struck me that I could choose my friends. I mean it seems pretty obvious, right? But it really felt like an epiphany at the time, and I felt empowered. Going forward, I began to focus more on the friends who were bringing out the best in me, and who were creating a progressive environment for me. Ultimately, things started falling into place. Soon I found myself living in a world I could grow in!"

"I have one other story," Lucas continued. "My final year of high school got off to a terrible start. I was distracted by my social life and was paying little or no attention to my studies. I was lying to my parents about my grades and my attendance. As the first half of the year drew closer to an end, I knew that I was doomed to fail. I was terrified to talk to my parents about what was going on, and I expected a horrific reaction from them once I broke the news. But finally I bit the bullet and decided to own up to my father about what was going on. To my surprise, he showed a lot of understanding and gave me the support I needed to get back on track. I knew I wasn't in it alone anymore, and felt I owed it to myself and to my father to get my act together. Believe it or not, I ended up graduating that year with top grades. I wonder what would have been if I hadn't honored my integrity by getting honest with my father that day."

quest for meaning

I find that my own thoughts on *integrity* inevitably turn to the question "what is my life *really* about?" This question points to the *hunger for meaning* that lies at the heart of human longing. Yet so often we find ourselves immersed in a false reality that breeds dead-end experiences of meaninglessness. As a consequence, our vital energies quickly become depleted, and illness or depression frequently follow. Truly, when our lives are lacking a reference to genuine purpose, we feel empty, anxious, lost, lifeless.

In this present era, to say the least, we are riding a wave of tumultuous change. This results in a great deal of confusion about personal directions of meaning. We find ourselves somewhat disoriented, distracted, if not at times, totally out of sync with the deeper purposes of life. Disillusionment ensues when meaning is absent – it reveals a disconnection from our own inner truth.

To some degree, unresolved tensions between *meaning* and *mediocrity* play out in the different stages of our lives. They are felt as an inner disquiet, a sense of not being right with ourselves. This is when we often hear a call to authenticity. As we embrace and commit ourselves to a journey of integrity, we come in touch with vital energies of life deep inside ourselves. Increased strength of purpose enables us to overcome fear and self-doubt, and to progressively dissolve the destructive anxiety of meaninglessness.

The dynamics of personal decline (inattention, image-making, indecisiveness) signal the need to identify sources of disintegration (*dis-integrity*) in our lives that are run interference on self-actualization. Through an ongoing enlargement of awareness, we are able to unmask the limiting beliefs and deceptive strivings that hold us captive to fear. We are then able to awaken new intention and make decisive choices in accord with our core values.

An experience of awakening is a moment of self-recognition when one is graced with deeper insight into the path and purpose of one's life. Such revelations imply a transformed vision of where one's life wants to go. They fortify individual integrity by placing focus on essential meaning.

One way I try to provoke conscious intention is to confront myself with some challenging questions related to essential meaning. How open am I to change – how willing to explore possibilities not yet imagined? Am I living the life I love, with my primary focus on what matters most? Am I giving expression to my deepest passions? Am I drawing forth my capacity for creativity and love, and developing my unique talents to benefit others? What form of human suffering is awaiting my compassion? Am I playing life for high enough stakes, or walking in shoes that are too small? How can my life make a bigger difference to the common good?

"What does authenticity ask of me?" perhaps best sums up all of the above questions. Each of us is called to set forth on our own hero journey, to undergo a particular set of challenges, and create our own original life. Awakenings give us the energy and vision to jump into the adventure of that creation – any significant leap of meaning enables us to meet difficult trials and advance our lives forward.

wholesome intention

Right direction in one's life can be found, or otherwise, we seem to get lost in a lot of confused misdirections. Without true intention, we just go through the motions. Where there is no direction of meaning and no enlargement of self, identity becomes somewhat frozen. Only as we become attuned to our core values do we find a congruence with our deepest potential and with a path that is in accord with our true purpose.

Conscious intention steadies the way forward – as our motivations undergo critique, purification, and refinement, we progressively surrender the one-sided ego to the creative purposes of the universe. The exercise of such intent helps to override the ego's aggressive pursuit of personal satisfactions, and to weed out the biases that keep us locked in the darkness of self-indulgence. Cosmologist Brian Swimme speaks about transforming the basis of one's vision from self-interest to service: from the ego-bound world – desire and fear, ignorance and greed, addiction to profit, prejudice and rivalry, excessive affections – to the spiritual, the deep, the energetic, the eternal aspects.

In this manner, integrity finds new depth. As we become more keenly sensitive to the needs of others, i.e. moving beyond an exclusive and obsessive attention to self, we sacrifice private gratifications for the well-being of others. Each expression of generosity attunes us to the reality of human interconnection, giving us an expanded sense of belonging and drawing us into a larger story of meaning. As we reframe our intentions, we strengthen our capacity to act and to create.

When I look back over the years, I recognize that many clues were given to guide my path through life – threads of meaning that weave together the seemingly incoherent elements of my life biography. The nurturing of a keen desire for authenticity has been the cornerstone of my integrity, creating an aliveness that even now seems to gather steam as it goes.

One thing is certain, there is no end to self-development. The more I age, the more I feel compelled to push towards further horizons of meaning. In the end, I know I will never figure my life out – I hope only to become ever more at home in the mystery of my being. One meaning that rings most true for me is that happiness expands exponentially as we come to realize that our unique life purpose is connected to something much greater than oneself.

Integrity and intention walk hand in hand. To live intentionally is to surrender to a vision of what one's life might become when one allows the blind, narrow, ego-made world to yield to an expanded truth of meaning. Then, one's life purpose moves its focus from the private to the common good, where pride of personal achievement gives way to an outward generosity of spirit.

Careful discernment enables us to identify more precisely what adds to or subtracts value from our lives. Thorough appraisals of value help us unmask and discard unwholesome intention. The greater our moral clarity, the better able we are to choose wise courses of actions.

Awakening is never once and for all, but recurs again and again as one's vision and understanding evolve. Intentional practices of wisdom, kindness, compassion, equanimity, and gratitude help create a world that does not yet exist. Personal integrity is based upon choosing how we want to live, and designing environments that support and strengthen our power of intention.

Lucas had a few final thoughts to offer: "I can relate value-based integrity directly to my work. In construction, we speak about the structural integrity of a building. When one element of a building is weak or missing, it compromises the strength of the entire structure. In my job I manage a team of workers in different sub-trades. One trade relies on the other, and they work in tandem to bring the job together like the inner workings of a watch or an engine. When each worker contributes his or her expertise, the highest quality is achieved."

"The same can be said for personal integrity. When one virtue or value is weak or missing, it resonates through our entire life, and undermines our force of character. I may, for example, value communication in order to form strong friendships and business relationships, but if I don't value punctuality, I may put those relationships at risk. I may value exercise, but if I don't value healthy eating habits, I miss out on a total health benefit. So we need an integral value system to build personal integrity. If there is a weak link, it will undermine the strength of the whole."

Earlier in our conversation, Lucas shared that from time to time he reflects upon what makes one's life fulfilled. In his words: "I have sometimes thought about what kind of legacy I would like to leave. It is important to ask yourself who you want to be, how you would like to be remembered, and what are your defining characteristics?" Following up on this statement, I could not resist asking Lucas how he himself would like to be held in memory. He paused to reflect for a moment, and then replied,

"Thoughtful, caring, compassionate, understanding, forgiving – a combination of all of these."

"Integrity is wisdom. Acting with integrity is embracing the ideals that you are striving towards. Real wisdom includes action, not just knowledge. I get frustrated when my actions go against my values, when I act without virtue."

6. THE PRACTICE OF PRESENCE

Waking up means we turn our attention on the being happening now, and realize how this experience here now - this being embodied, this having a mind, this consciousness being experienced now – is absolutely new, fresh, strange, mysterious, vivid … the present moment escaping all the time, and this moment new also all the time.

Pascal Auclair

The moment one gives close attention to anything, even a blade of grass, it becomes a mysterious, awesome, indescribably magnificent world in itself.

Henry Miller

As you quiet your mind, you begin to see the nature of your own resistance, your stuckness, more clearly.
You see the mental struggles, inner dialogues, self-narrations, the ways you procrastinate or resist life changes.
Don't try to change the patterns; just notice them.
As you cultivate the witness, things change. You don't have to change them. When you're being here now, in loving awareness, things just change

Ram Dass

being with what is

Heather had a schooling in meditation while teaching in Korea as a young adult. Tutored by a Buddhist nun, she cultivated a practice of *sitting* in silence. "Meditation is one way of becoming aware of the movements in your mind. It points towards detachment from mental disturbances and distractions. At the bottom of a pond, the water is not moving, and meditation seeks to bring us to a place of non-movement in the mind."

Heather was eager to say more about the meaning of her meditation practice: "Pure presence is being with your experience just as it is. You are not trying to change what is happening, to control or resist it. There are things going on that you do not want to *sit* with. It takes courage to sit with what is. When you do, it loses its power over you. In fact, your resistance to what is, is the cause of your distress."

Heather Evans

"Sometimes you think that thinking about something is paying attention to it and dealing with it. But this is the thinking mind, not the awareness mind. Suppose anger comes up in your experience, and you ask: how am I going to take care of my anger? Rather than pushing it away or pulling it in, you need to see it for what it is. When you see your anger to the core, when you see it fully, it no longer has power to control you."

I asked Heather if this has been the case in her own practice. "At the meditation center in Korea, there was one experience I recall that was particularly revelatory. I had been meditating regularly, and at the same time I was going through a lot of relationship difficulties. When feelings of insecurity are triggered, I feel very vulnerable. In that situation, I wanted to connect and try to resolve the conflict in order to get out of the enormous amounts of insecurity I was feeling. My partner, on the other hand, had internalized the conflict, and was pushing me away."

"This led to a pivotal breakthrough. My teacher had earlier introduced the technique of being with pain, and during my very first sitting meditation, I was experiencing a lot of tingling sensations and pain in my leg, and some numbness as well. I simply watched the sensations, and noted them, and eventually they all stopped. If you mindfully observe your inner distress, without judging it or thinking about it, a funny thing happens – it eventually just goes away."

Heather further reflected: "I was going through a lot of emotional turmoil, and again a lot of insecurity came up. It was so strong! I had a lot of heaviness in my chest. But I just kept meditating. I had been instructed to just note the sensations, not analyze or judge or interpret my experience. Just be aware, be present, but do not stop the experience. Rather note the sensations as they are in the present moment. And strangely these feelings washed through me, and then stopped."

"I allowed these feelings to come out in full force, probably demonstrating to my subconscious that when insecurity comes up, I don't have to be scared. At deeper levels of meditation, you understand the cause, you see the beginning and the end of what is moving through your mind. This provides a good lesson in the impermanence of experience."

"Inherent in suffering," Heather continued, "is the notion that pain shouldn't be there. With pain, you assume that something is wrong, that it shouldn't be happening. Though you can't avoid pain, you can minimize the suffering that comes with not accepting and allowing and experiencing everything that is happening in each moment. But what I have found to help the most is self-acceptance, learning to befriend your total experience. Instead of trying to shut out negative thoughts and feelings, give them a hug. Welcome them as guests, create a space for them until they are ready to leave."

"Good practice leads to informed action. When you get off your meditation mat, and walk into the world, your eyes are open in a new way and you see things with greater clarity, and you act with more awareness."

the emerging moment

Primary awareness begins with a quality of keen attention to one's life experience from moment to moment. What is going on right here, right now? *Now* is brand new – I have never been in this moment before. And this moment is now vanishing!

The challenge of mindfulness is to engage oneself in a discipline of self-observation that connects us to the web of our experience. We bring our attention to biological, mental, and spiritual processes that reveal the world inside ourselves. We also witness what is happening in the external environment in which we are situated, attuning ourselves to person and place, and the pulse of outer stimuli.

The game is to *hang out* with ourselves, and take time to notice as much as we can through a practice of alert wide-eyed attention to our immediate experience. Sight, sound, smell, taste, and touch create avenues of awareness that monitor whatever is being received from the outer world. Inner consciousness notices the pulse of the psyche – feelings and fantasies, memories and longing, pleasure and pain, desire and aversion.

A tutored habit of inward attention helps us monitor a whole gamut of subjective experiences: biological, sensual, sexual, psychological, emotional, inspirational, ethical. Thereby we come in touch with our intrinsic beauty and goodness, and awaken a new appreciation of value and meaning. We too meet suffering and pain, and get to witness our ego in the dance of its self-assertion.

If we are open to each emerging moment, a habit of self-observation gives us the data of raw experience. We notice ourselves feeling cold, angry, lonely, hungry, joyful, jealous, tired, blissful. We notice our behaviours, our relationships, and the roles we play. Exactly what is happening is always waiting to be noticed.

Commonly, however, we tend to jump into the interpretation of personal experience without an adequate quantity and quality of self-observation. Primary awareness precedes any interpretations of experience – its task is to describe rather than to define experience; to acknowledge the data of experience with complete attention before analyzing it. We need to *be with* our personal experience in a deeply mindful way before we try to figure ourselves out or make sense of what is going on. As Heather suggested: give the thinking mind a rest.

evasion of depth

No matter how much we commit ourselves to the way of attention, there are still large aspects of human experience that remain unconscious. Different words describe the darkness of our unknowing: repression, avoidance, denial, evasion, distraction, blind spots.

Indeed, we filter reality in and out, and give ourselves reasons for not noticing what is going on in our experience. It follows that there are challenging questions to ask ourselves: What are we avoiding?

Are certain habits of distraction diverting our attention to superficial reality? Have we allowed ourselves to get caught up in too much triviality? What defensive postures have we put in place to censor parts of our experience that we do not want to deal with?

Jesuit scholar Bernard Lonergan describes different biases of consciousness that limit our *seeing* and leave us with big blind spots. There is vested short-sighted self-interest that filters reality in order to promote private advantage for oneself or one's group. This is the ego in pursuit of its own narcissistic satisfactions, where the needs of others become invisible. Also there is the flight from insight, when enquiry shuts down and the discipline of learning is refused – the importance of scientific and philosophical knowledge is downplayed, often even belittled.

The last restriction of consciousness that Lonergan describes is dramatic bias, a spontaneous exclusion of psychic content that is too painful to admit to consciousness. Often born out traumas of deep wounding, this censorship of experience is the most difficult to undo.

Repression is a coping mechanism that allows us to block out painful memories of the past, or that closes down one's awareness of the existence of impulses and behaviours one does not want to admit, even to oneself. The problem with repression is that what is banished from awareness gets buried inside ourselves where it remains alive and active. Psychologist Carl Jung suggests that what is not brought to consciousness comes to us as fate.

One might push envy out of awareness, only later to act out rage towards those bitterly resented. Or, one may try to put on a brave face and bury sadness, only later to undergo physical symptoms resulting from unresolved grief. Similarly, experiences of greed or lust or anger that are denied may eventually turn up in abusive behaviours. In the language of psychology, these are called autonomous complexes. They have a life of their own.

On the other hand, to the extent that we can befriend ourselves just as we are, we gain a more complete mastery of self. The spiritual writer Sebastian Moore makes a distinction between repression and restriction: repression denies the power of negative drives and leaves certain impulses unchecked, whereas restriction acknowledges what is experienced, however negative and distasteful, and decides how to contain negative energies in such a way as to not violate oneself or others.

In other words, cognizance of one's experience empowers self-control – our task is then to find a positive way to channel negative energy, and to discard inappropriate behaviours and damaging projections.

In order to undo repression, idealized self-images that attach themselves to perfection need to be discarded. As we acknowledge the muddy world inside ourselves that we would rather not have to think about, we connect to ourselves in a more truthful manner. By getting our hands into the *mud*, we begin to cultivate a garden, coaxing the expression of our true goodness. Flowers do grow out of mud!

negotiating the unknown

The absence of self-presence feeds a dynamic of personal decline. Through inattentiveness and bias, denial and distraction, we restrict our horizon of self-knowledge, and limit our range of insight and action. What we do not see hurts us.

A partnership with the inner world allows us to open ourselves up to the hidden contents of the unconscious. The role of consciousness is to integrate what is coming up from the unconscious – to discover buried emotions, to address inner conflict, to be attentive to symbolic imagery, to connect with deep intention. What is pushing into awareness is significant – as we breathe with the unconscious, we open ourselves to our own transformative potential.

Symbolic images call forth deeper levels of awareness that connect us to a new depth of reality. Acts of imagination open up a path towards personal potentiality. To access the intelligence rooted in the unconscious we need to access the data of the world inside ourselves. Images arising from the unconscious point the way to greater authenticity. They carry the visionary elements that portray the emergent meaning of one's life. Symbols bring us into contact with our inner depths to reveal our extraordinary possibilities. The more we learn to feel and talk to the images that spontaneously present themselves, the better we are able to discern an authentic path for ourselves.

If we become entrenched in our emotional routines and habits of thought, we are not in reality – the psyche then writes its own biography. A quality of consciousness is realized only as we free ourselves from the grip of unconscious complexes and negative mental states. Beyond automatic reactivity, we are able to re-pattern experience.

Psychic transformation, as described by author Robert Doran, is a process whereby we can turn the noise of our psyche into song. This task of transformation starts with a cultivated attentiveness to what the psyche is revealing. The practice of self-presence enables us to gather the data of our inner and outer experience, to enter into a dialogue with the psychic data, and move from reaction to intentional action.

In this way, rather than being swallowed up by the unconscious flow of negative energy, we are able to break free from the emotional confinements that run interference on our power of self-determination. We then can write our true and unique biography.

In order to bring one's power of presence to a new level, Heather emphasizes that mindfulness practices, like any other skill, require a discipline of learning similar to the way an athlete's talent is honed through rigorous training. Based upon her own committed journey of meditation, Heather draws a parallel between self-nurture and self-giving: "What inspires my practice of self-presence is not something

I do just for myself – it is a gift for everyone. Presence translates into every interaction you have with others. We are always in a dance between the internal and external. My practice is creating me, and changing the world around me at the same time."

"Good practice leads to informed action. When you get off your meditation mat, and walk into the world, your eyes are open in a new way and you see things with greater clarity, and you act with more awareness."

7. QUESTIONS IN MOTION

In any conversation the person who asks the questions shapes the dialogue.
Sam Keen

Genuineness ... does not brush questions aside, smother doubts, push problems down, escape to activity, to chatter, to passive entertainment, to sleep, to narcotics. It confronts issues, inspects them, studies their many aspects, works out their various implications, contemplates their concrete consequences in one's own life and in the lives of others.
Bernard Lonergan

*I have no special talents.
I am only passionately curious.*
Albert Einstein

the question man

Mike says he has never stopped asking questions since the age of three, and well deserves being branded *the question man*. As I began to question Mike about the art of asking, he firstly emphasized the difference between small questions and big ones. "There are small questions that point to the choices we make on a day-to-day basis. These questions require more immediate answers that form a basis for practical decisions of action."

"Big questions are the ones that occupy me most of the time: What am I doing with my life? Why am I here? What is really important to me? How can I love, and how can I grow?" Mike said that he began to focus on *questions of meaning* at the age of seventeen. "These essential questions don't go away, they are never completely resolved. You live these questions."

Mike Abravanel

It is no wonder that Mike is making a career of personal coaching. His motivation is to help others walk their own unfolding path. Mike is quick to emphasize that "there is no path to follow, only the one you create." I asked him how questions factored into making a path, to which he replied: "What I have noticed in my own life is that the questions that I ask compel the steps I take. They open up new pathways."

Mike had more to say about coaching: "Asking powerful questions is considered to be one of a coach's core competencies. Those who come to me are predominantly looking for answers. As a coach, my major task is to ask questions that elicit new insight, to create more space in which to move, and to open up larger frameworks of meaning that guide one's courses of action. I help individuals to see their blind spots, and their biases that block larger awareness. I encourage them to avoid coming to decisions too quickly, and to take more time to find the right questions, the questions that really matter."

I checked in with Mike to see if he was getting tired of all my questions! "Bring me more," he said. I added these two last queries: "What does a good question look like?" and "What do you mean when you say a question is something you live?" To the first, Mike summed up: "A good question is open-ended, it generates possibility, it does not lead to a particular answer or outcome. It enlarges one's perspective, and explores wider meaning and value."

Then, in response to my second query, Mike expressed what it meant personally for him to live his questions: "When I am asking myself a new question, I feel a tension in my body. I go into a chaotic space inside myself where there is no up and no down. I am in an unknown place that makes me feel very uncomfortable. In time, out of the dark unknown, an intimation, a spark, a word, an image appears ... it's hard, but I try to stay right there, and allow more sparks to come up before taking any next steps. What I am saying is that my whole being is involved: I feel the question, I think it, I dream it. It is important to stay with the question, rather than grab for an answer. When you let the process happen, there comes a moment when there is an opening, a moment of clarity."

"Then I will write my insight into words, or express it in some art form. Beyond that, I share my emerging awareness with others, and invite feedback. From the first question I asked have come sub-questions and new answers, which themselves beg further questions. I have learned it's not good to hold onto any answer too tightly."

self-enquiry

It seems to be a rule that we grow in the direction of the questions we ask. For questions run in front of insights – they set a process of enquiry in motion. To evoke ever greater awareness, we pose endless questions – this fosters the emergence of imagination and intention. An open life is guided by questions that probe what we do not yet know. Certainly, it is sometimes very hard to let the questions lead us to where they want to bring us.

Self-enquiry resides within a context of emergent meaning – we wonder about who we are, and why we are here. And so we engage personal experience, embarking on a journey of self-discovery that is lived as a question, an experiment, a discipline of enquiry and critical reflection, an advance towards self-realization. Further questions are always waiting to be asked. Further questions lead to deeper insight, deeper insight to sounder judgment, and sounder judgment to more meaningful action.

As we have seen when discussing *presence*, primary awareness entails a witness of concrete lived experience – biological, emotional, intellectual, aesthetic, spiritual. On its heels, reflective awareness begins a dialogue with the data of one's experience, in order to find intelligible patterns within that experience – this is an attempt to understand as much as one can about why what is happening is happening. Self-enquiry focuses on the raw data of inner and outer experience – we try to make some sense of it. The better our grasp of self-understanding, the greater our self-mastery. For reflective awareness empowers us to act, rather than live reactively. It creates the basis for making prudent decisions and acting wisely.

Unfortunately, and all too frequently, we satisfy ourselves with easy explanations that short-circuit awareness. The common tendency is to look for quick answers. But when we are in a hurry to figure things out, we oversimplify the complexity of human experience and let certain questions that have been never been asked remain unasked. Awareness is always incomplete, and so instead of ready answers, we need to hold the tension of our questions longer, as well as search for better questions to ask.

Life never stands still, and so self-observation and inner reflection never cease. Each moment brings new experience, begs steady attention, and draws forth further understanding. Though personal identity undergoes continuous revision, we always meet within ourselves a certain amount of resistance to redefining our self-images and modifying long-held habits of thinking and acting.

Our range of insight hinges on our openness to emerging truth. Ultimately, what we know cannot be frozen, locked down, or dogmatized. Thus, our *conclusions* should be tentative, rather than absolute – for greater awareness always lies beyond our immediate reach. Acknowledging the gaps in our self-knowledge prompts us to look for those questions we are avoiding that need to be asked.

When insights do occur, they seem to arrive somewhat gratuitously – though they are often the fruit of a long task of enquiry. There is great excitement, and relief, whenever we *see the light*. When an idea clicks, when something dawns on us, when we comprehend a pattern of personal experience, we feel joyful and more relaxed.

As insights accumulate, they help refine the understanding we have of ourselves and the world we inhabit. But even as we deepen self-understanding and acquire a new clarity of self-insight, we are again and again thrown back into the unknown. The process of continuous self-discovery always challenges us to live inside bigger questions.

In the modern era, certainly we are moving away from the classicist model where knowledge was seen as static – old doctrines, frozen beliefs, certitudes of knowing. Now a greater emphasis is placed on subjective learning – allowing new insights to ride piggyback on older wisdom. Beyond once-and-for-all truths lies vast uncharted territory. We are learning to appreciate what-we-do-not-know as much as what-we-do-know, and thereby, put forth only probable interpretations of reality.

emotional authenticity

Chinese medicine advocates that we beware of two dangers: climate and the emotions. Indeed, a key component of self-enquiry lies in the cultivation of emotional literacy – the ability to read and interpret our emotions. The relaxed awareness of our feelings allows us to explore the stories they tell, and point us to the values that they reveal.

Self-awareness begins with taking cognizance of our feelings as they arise in each new moment of our lives. We often want to run away from our feelings, narcotize them, push them down, or dismiss them altogether. But on the other side of denial, the way of attention empowers us keep a close ear to our feelings.

Feelings are neither good or bad, they just are. Denying a feeling does not make it go away. Feelings are not dangerous in themselves, but if they remain unrecognized they take on a life of their own and, in fact, can do an awful lot of damage. In fact, disowned feelings start to run the show and define our deeds. And they tend to generate truly negative consequences.

One has only to think of the projections we throw at one another, our defensive scapegoating, and the wide range of our behaviours rooted in violence.

The deconstruction of violence begins with keen attentiveness to the experience of one's own emotional experience. Beyond repression or the acting out of our feelings, we ought to listen with reverence to what our emotions have to say – all feelings reveal value. In this way, we are able to recognize and withdraw harmful projections, and avoid some of the potential harm that we might otherwise inflict upon ourselves and others.

Growth in wisdom allows us to embrace and value emotions we once denied. Fear, for example, is a useful emotion – it signals danger, either real or imagined, and warns us of potential menace. If the danger is real, we can get out of harm's way. But when fear is based only on imagined danger, we need to discern the unreal nature of what seemed threatening, and then let it go. Guilt can also be described as a healthy emotion. For our conscience is not there to torment us, but to instruct our hearts. It invites us to live in congruence with the truth that will set us free. Pathological guilt, on the other hand, grows in the soil of repression feeding a poverty of self-awareness.

There are other examples: self-pity has been described as a new wind blowing through the soul – asking us to take care of ourselves; sadness, a pure human emotion, highlights the lost bliss of meaningful experience – begging us to work through the grief we feel; anger reveals injustice and injury – acting as a powerful catalyst to foster justice and reconciliation.

As Jungian psychologist James Hollis has pointed out, no prisons are more confining than those that we do not know we are in. Through cultivating emotional literacy, no matter what feelings arise, we are able to liberate ourselves from the tyranny of the unconscious, thereby expanding our capacity to choose and to act wisely.

a larger truth

We are more than passive observers of self. As we cultivate self-intimacy, one's purpose and potential is revealed – who we really are emerges out of a truthful encounter with self that requires a depth of courage and commitment. The joyful experience of authenticity one never imagined accrues from our steady practices of attention and intention.

Such a journey of self-awakening can best described as an interlocking set of practices: self-observation, self-enquiry, and self-understanding working together to build a momentum of learning that supports our progressive evolution. Questions and insights manifest in mysterious ways, arising from our deep passion to know where we stand and where we want to go.

Integrative knowing involves matter and mind, language and symbol, abstract thinking and artistic intuition. Through different modes of emerging consciousness, the hidden universe inside ourselves is revealed. A combination of body-mind-spirit practices guides us to the questions that want to lead us into a larger unified field of truth.

Our learning is also interpersonal. As we engage one another and explore our inter-subjective experience, we are born in the encounters we have with others. This involves shared enquiry, insight, and action. The whole expresses itself in each individual, but the self we discover is not separate – one's emerging story and one's potential of meaning are found in reference to an interconnected whole.

That is to say, the story of any one individual is a story within a bigger story.

More and more, we are relying on interdependent investigations of truth, and learning a keen respect for the discoveries of others. New models of collaborative enquiry enable us to see through an ever-wider lens, and to acquire interdisciplinary knowledge from varied wellsprings of scientific discovery, artistic insight, and spiritual wisdom.

There is no full grasp of truth – we have only approximate understandings of our vast and highly complex universe. Any interpretations of reality point to probabilities, not certainties. Our frameworks of understanding describe reality, but can never explain it definitively. In the long curve of time, the evolutionary leap of consciousness supports the emergence of mysteries of life.

So we act on what we know, opt for genuine value, and then wait for the next question. In this regard, Mike suggests that the biggest way to influence content is through the process. "When those I coach get excited about the answers they are discovering, I ask them to reflect on their questioning process, and how they came up with their answers. If the process is faulty, the answer will be off the mark. But when the process is on the mark, there is genuine openness, a readiness to explore new possibilities, an attentiveness to all the signs. You don't jump to conclusions too quickly, you listen to the wind and the stars and your friends, but in the end, you interpret all the data very carefully, and take responsibility for your the choices you make."

"When I am asking myself a new question, I feel a tension in my body. I go into a chaotic space inside myself where there is no up and no down. I am in an unknown place that makes me feel very uncomfortable."

8. The Art of Discernment

*Some people will never learn anything, for this reason,
because they understand everything too soon.*
Alexander Pope

*Beings endowed with self-awareness become,
precisely in virtue of that bending back upon themselves,
immediately capable of rising into a new sphere of existence:
in truth another world is born.*
Teilhard de Chardin

*The only way to make the right decision
is to know what the wrong decision is.*
Paulo Coelho

knowing what is true

Jen says that her role as a holistic health practitioner is to help empower individuals to actualize their full potential of health and wellness. "The initial step is to listen to your body, to watch it, to feel it, to approach it with curiosity. Your body is asking for attention – it wants you to look into it."

"I emphasize to my clients that healing takes time – it is a process that requires patience, like the dripping of water that transforms stone over time. In fact, living life in a hurry is often what has put them in a situation of needing help and healing. These days, we want answers right away, we don't like waiting for a thorough diagnosis. Everybody expects an instant fix, a one-session solution."

Jen went on to further describe her role: "I listen to a client give an account of their experience, and then look at what their body is telling me. With a combination of knowledge and wisdom, I identify as best I can what is going on physically, mentally, emotionally and energetically. This invites the question of how the body and the mind are communicating with each other, and what that manifests in the present moment. After zoning in on specific issues, I then zone out to the big picture to evaluate my client's health as a whole."

Jen Wende

"As a healing guide, I bring my insight, my awareness, and my curiosity into each encounter. I bring an outside perspective, and try to empower clients to find their own awareness. I stress the importance of really getting to know oneself, and seeing one's own patterns of experience."

"Most of the time we live in tiny bubbles of knowing. We are afraid of the unknown. We are afraid to ask questions that have answers we don't want to hear. Most of all, I try to help my clients get more curious about the big picture. There is a lot we know, but there is a lot more we don't know."

Jen continued: "It is so vital to keep curiosity alive. When you are curious, you want to gain new knowledge that opens new doors. There is always more to learn, more doors to open. One needs to learn what one does not understand. The moment you stop being curious, there is no moving forward, no enquiry, no further insight. You get stuck in your first answers."

"Supposing you have an experience of pain in the body: you need to focus on the pain, but you also need to explore the body as a whole to see where the pain is originating from. You need to look for the bigger picture, get a better understanding of the nature of the pain. Stop, remove yourself from the situation, take a breath – you always need to keep checking in with yourself. Listen to your body sensations. Are they expansive, or constrictive? Look with the eyes of the heart."

"Misdiagnosis results when we get attached to one interpretation of what's going on, and do not take a look at all the information that needs to be recognized. We don't acknowledge the limits of our interpretations, or how we sometimes completely misinterpret our experience." Jen adds a further thought: "We also need to discern where there are shortcomings in self-understanding. All too often we stay fixated in the little picture."

"The majority of the people I see who have pain issues have not had an *official* accident, which is to say they weren't hit by a car, or didn't fall off a ladder. They usually describe the occurrence as one of my clients did: 'I went to tie my shoe and my back just gave out'. He thought that the act of tying a shoe was the cause of his back pain. The reality is that backs don't give out from tying shoelaces – such an injury can result from years of poor alignment, and other health issues. In this instance, perhaps some burden of stress was the straw that broke this camel's back. By focusing too closely on the little picture, we can miss the big picture."

I asked Jen to elaborate on this little-picture big-picture question. "Pride of knowing can get in the way – we need to be right, and might be heard saying, 'I definitely know what I am talking about.' Pride can keep us in our tiny bubbles of *knowing*. We are convinced that we have the right take on what's happening, and deny that there is lots going on that we don't see or understand. The problem then boils down to: we don't know that we don't know."

"Taking this further, false pride masks one's fear of facing reality. Our take on reality is filtered through our fears. We fixate on our narrow answers – when our minds are attached to particular explanations, we do not allow for something new to emerge beyond what we presently understand or imagine reality to be. By *explaining* rather than *exploring* ourselves, we stay in the little picture."

To get beyond our one-sided subjective perspectives, Jen suggests: "We need to be open to surprises. The land of exploration is the most beautiful place to be. There are no final answers: we must test what we have come to know, and then seek further insight."

dynamics of deception

Even as we strive diligently to comprehend what we do not understand, we are very often mistaken in our knowing. This makes it necessary to put our understanding and judgment to the test before taking decisive action. Bernard Lonergan makes the point that insights are a dime a dozen – we have them all the time, but how can we be certain that we have a *right* take on reality. Any insight – rational, intuitive, artistic, spiritual – should never go unquestioned.

Certainly, the truth of new ideas needs to be authenticated – their accuracy questioned, and errors of understanding weeded out. The validity of an insight requires verification against what we already think to be true. So often when we seem to know what we are talking about, it acts as a cover up for our lack of understanding.

To know is to understand correctly – a conjunction of attention, enquiry, and critical reflection. Discernment, a third level of awareness that follows the observation and interpretation of experience, is integral to the process of knowing. With careful discernment, one increases the probability of getting a good grasp on what is really true.

When does truth go off the rails? An incompleteness of attention in the witness of one's own inner and outer experience can lead to bias, inaccurate observation, sketchy data, guessing, false assumptions, and many an oversight. More often than not, there is the tendency to rush to interpret experience. And so we arrive at hurried conclusions, and reduce our self-understanding to oversimplified explanations. The more we rush, the more rash our judgments – the choices we make suffer from a lack of deep listening and careful reflection.

A splinter in one's foot can cause a lot of grief. So too a single blind spot, a wrong assumption, a small oversight can throw us right off track. What is missing in our awareness limits the range of actions that we undertake. As long as we pretend to know everything there is to know, or minimize the need to know more than we do, we become ever more stuck in narrow-mindedness.

Though we may never have a full certainty about truth, we come closer to its realization with enhanced attention, cumulative insight, and sound judgment. A committed practice of mindfulness helps us become keenly attuned to personal experience. Beyond self-observation, enquiry and discernment help us attain wise insight that puts us on a path of prudent action.

thorough learning

The challenge of authenticity invites us to create a life that is congruent with our boundless possibilities. This entails a journey of self-discovery that brings us into the recognition of our true nature – it asks for a commitment to thorough learning.

Learning often occurs in fits and starts. When we are on our game, we question experience, develop new insights, and exercise sound judgment. When we are off our game, we lack self-presence, distract attention, flee insight, and become victims of our own rash judgment. If we are honest with ourselves, we can take a look at how prone we are to laziness in learning, and how readily we turn away from the task of awareness.

Any constriction of consciousness brings with it a measure of limitation and suffering, and subtracts happiness from our lives. On the other hand, continuous learning progressively liberates us from ignorance and error – we discover more truth, and therefore, more freedom.

The questions we ask and the judgments we exercise in regard to *value* are integral to personal development. With sustained attentiveness to our day-to-day experience, we become empowered to assess what is truly worthwhile in our lives as opposed to what simply seems to be so. As a scientist puts a hypothesis under rigorous scrutiny, so too our evaluations about the authentic human good must be put to the test.

In this way, we catch rationalizations of what is, in fact, detrimental to our own good. This allows us to become better attuned to our true needs. Uninformed opinions and rash judgments can be exposed and carefully critiqued, enabling us to break out of our habitual interpretations of value in order to discern our genuine well-being.

Genuineness is about living our questions, coming to terms with self-deception, and unceasingly straining forwards towards higher value. To avoid fast answers, we need to stay with our sometimes stubborn questions, and resist throwing simple explanations at the complexity of our lived human experience. Skilful discernment leads us to challenge common non-sense, and boosts our confidence in the good that we come to affirm.

Indeed, learning is a patient sport. It takes time to observe, question, and reflect in front of our actions. Slow time allows us to be fully present to what is happening, and to better understand what is truly needed at any one moment. It enables us to move from the shallow interpretation of our experience and from superficial evaluations of meaning into a depth of awareness and freedom.

discriminating intention

Our intentions are unstable – they waver between noble purpose and short-sighted self-interest. Certainly, we are drawn by both darkness and light, and so must learn how to discriminate between the two. How can we find genuine value, as opposed to being trapped by fear, ignorance, and greed?

The reckless ego affirms its own deception, shunning prudent intention. The ego puts satisfactions before value. Our minds must relinquish their attachment to what supports our private comfort in service of the wider human good. Wisdom invites us to ask the right questions in order to discriminate between motives – it helps us make the hard choice to forego immediate gratifications in favour of long-term value.

The task of authenticity is ongoing moral transformation: the development of a personal ethos which learns to distinguish carefully between what adds true value to life, and what robs it of meaning. Moral truth evolves as we develop our capacity to make our experience more intelligible. We are asked to challenge the good that we think we know or want to believe in, in order to find out not what seems to be real, but what is truly real.

Breakthroughs come about as we dare this adventure of freedom, a journey that releases us from the grip of deep-rooted complexes and boxed-in biases; and takes us beyond moral impotence. To think and act and speak truthfully requires moral courage. Each spiritual leap brings us into a deeper realization of bliss.

Indeed, we are saved by wisdom – it teaches us truth in the heart, and guides us in the way of the true good. Growth in self-knowledge allows us to recognize the selfish intentions that divorce us from wise understanding. Wisdom bestows on us the gift of prudence by which we unmask self-deception, and thereby empower right action. Indeed, wise understanding is the antidote to misguided judgment and faulty reasoning. It is through discernment that we move beyond ego ambition into a world of meaning.

As I conversed with Jen, I could see the parallel between the method she employs to empower healing and the process of exploring personal vision. In a nutshell, Jen's healing practice includes: seeing what is happening energetically in the present time, zoning out to the big picture, keeping curiosity alive, investing the time it takes, identifying pain and pathology, cultivating self-knowledge, going beyond first answers and asking further questions, being open to surprise and committed to continuous exploration.

In seeking out human potential, the game is much the same: being attentive to what is actually happening in your life, acknowledging what's not working, seeking to understand why what's not working is not working, and keeping curiosity at the center of your life. Daring to embrace your genuine self also entails enlarging self-knowledge, unmasking false pride and other ego obstacles, practicing discernment to find your right path, and not least of all, being open to the unexpected.

For sure, this makes for pure adventure. Self-discovery knows no limits. In Jen's own words: "More truth is always ready to pop out. Through continuous exploration and growth, we become immersed in continuous discovery. There is always darkness upon which we can shed more light."

"There is always more to learn, more doors to open. One needs to learn what one does not understand. The moment you stop being curious, there is no moving forward, no enquiry, no further insight. You get stuck in your first answers."

9. WEB OF ERROR

We don't see things as they are, we see things as we are.
Anaïs Nin

The drifter has not yet found himself; he has not yet discovered his own deed and so is content to do what everyone else is doing; he has not yet discovered his own will and so he is content to choose what everyone else is choosing; he has not yet discovered a mind of his own and so he is content to think and say what everyone else is thinking and saying ...
Bernard Lonergan

If you don't make mistakes, you aren't really trying.
Coleman Hawkins

on the run

"I don't own my mistakes," admitted Barkley. "I can acknowledge them, but owning a mistake includes amending it. My pattern is trying to run away from my failures and disappointments, turning my back on what I know. I keep to the same game, and delude myself saying I will apply my awareness later – in other words, I am always making a run for it."

Barkley Cineus, Jr.

Barkley and I have had a conversation on the run for the past nine years since I first met him when he was nineteen. We have explored a lot of shadow territory together – one of our common refrains has been the importance of acknowledging and amending the errors we make along the way. When invited to put his voice into this book, Barkley tagged the web-of-error theme: "Sadly, I am still running. Sometimes I think I am growing, but it seems there are certain habits I can't shake. It's scary! I feel there is some deeper, darker part of me I'm scared of. I'm stuck running."

Curious about his pattern of escape, I interjected, "How do you run?" Barkley laughed: "Fast!!" After a short pause, he continued: "I want to be this great person, this powerful symbol of success, this icon, underdog in the rags-to-riches story, the bearer of truth."

I threw another question at Barkley, and asked him what was interfering with the achievement of his aspirations. "Deep-rooted fear! Over and over, I get caught in that web of errors. At times I think I've got things figured out, but I wake up and it feels like I am back at square zero, and I keep having to run. I keep trying to create my own hero story, but never live up to my noble goals. My actions are not in line with my values. When I don't like where the story is going, I change the story, I change the characters, I change the setting."

"Perhaps all this goes back to something I haven't dealt with – perhaps some fear-of-abandonment issues. I'll be in a story, and just the slightest hint that it's not going the way I wanted it to, then I am already looking for the exit. What I am running from is the feeling that I've disappointed someone. When people are disappointed in me, I fear potential abandonment. They realize that this guy is a fraud, and leave. My pattern has been to run at the first sign of their dissatisfaction with me. I know that I am not living up to expectations. Instead of bettering my performance, I move into another game."

"How," Barkley continued, "do you progress when every chance you have to better yourself, you always bail out? My pattern is to flee when I can't fake it any more. I create this bravado in my mind, a self-image to protect myself temporarily, a story that justifies what I am doing – but it only lasts for so long, and then it crumbles. In the end, there is no story to protect you. Once you become aware that you are running scared, it's hard to live with yourself because you can no longer lie to yourself. It's only easier to run until it's not easy to run!"

Barkley grimaced when asked for a concrete example, and then talked about his *running late* woes: "Here is the story of my life. I am late, late for everything. I hate hearing about it. I acknowledge it – it has been brought to my attention over and over again. Basically to say, I haven't changed my pattern. I have a hard time changing it, obviously. I'm not doing a good job. It's costing me. I am very defensive."

"Five minutes in my world is not the same as five minutes in the actual world," he further added. "I know why this kind of thing happens. I aim to please. I take on too much. I have a hard time framing events and encounters. I get stuck in one encounter, and fail to show up for the next. I try to justify this in my mind by saying I am here in the moment. I don't know how to create closure, and move on to the next event. I feel I am abandoning the person I am with, that I am disappointing them."

I asked him if a breakthrough was possible. "Absolutely!" was his quick response. "The more I talk about it, the more I face the issue. And increased understanding helps - the clearer I am about my lateness and why it persists, the better a handle I get on myself. Sometimes though, even when I do understand my behavior, I still give in to the old pattern. Another thing that is really helping me change more and more is having to face the consequences of my shortcomings. That's no fun!"

poverty of awareness

Errors multiply where there is more misunderstanding than understanding, more oversight than insight, and more inaction than daring to act. As we jump to conclusions, make assumptions, refuse feedback and constructive critique, we impair our ability to find a direction of true value and meaning.

The web of error gathers steam inasmuch as the past takes hold of us. Our tired behaviours repeat themselves over and over, and we remain stuck in the same habitual patterns of thinking, feeling, and (re)acting. Thereby, we are rendered powerless to one degree or another, unable to create the authentic story of our lives. In fact, there is no real story at all – we are being driven by complexes of psychic energy that have a life of their own.

A complex is energy that has constellated in the psyche based on our experiences of the past. In a sense, the psyche becomes grooved in a certain way, the result of patterns of experience and emotion learned in one's personal history. Until made conscious, we are owned by these psychological complexes, and forfeit our autonomy – we do not act, we react. And so, we are in captivity to the past. We may think we are acting in freedom, but in truth our choices are driven by learned behaviours. Only when these complexes are brought into the light of consciousness, can we meet our true selves, and begin to live inside the real biography of who we are.

A web of error is born in gaps found at each level of self-awareness – gaps in self-observation, self-reflection, and self-determination. Based on this, it becomes clear that inattention, misunderstanding, and indecisiveness set the dynamics of decline in motion and breed personal dysfunction. What are we not letting ourselves see?

At the level of primary awareness, we may fall asleep, or as Barkley tells, choose to run away. One's self-presence is compromised when we fail to be attentive to our subjective experience. Avoiding intimate self-encounter, we turn our attention to the trivial and overlook the essential. Any unwillingness to search for larger self-understanding takes a toll on our growth in self-awareness. Key insights are missed because some vital questions are brushed aside or never asked – as a result, self-development unfolds in slow motion.

the wrong way

In moments of discouragement and deep regret, often the question of what-went-wrong arises. Certainly, we make mistakes that contradict our true path, and leave us at odds with ourselves. Have we been carried along by wild illusions, or chased after distorted notions about where happiness is to be found? Have we been in the grip of unruly emotions or dull thoughts or mediocrity? Have we been punishing ourselves, or arguing for our limitations, or living inside a victim narrative? Have our lives been performance-driven in an attempt to overcome shame, deficiency, or woundings of the past? Have we become caught up in addictive behaviors as a way of managing our pain and anxiety?

The misreading of identity is perhaps another way we get it wrong. We might be trying to live in someone else's story, having not yet discovered our own deed. Bernard Lonergan suggests we have become *drifters* when we are doing and thinking what everyone else is doing and thinking, and not choosing for ourselves. Are we more defined from the outside in, than the inside out?

Context plays a role, and no doubt the noise and narcissism of contemporary culture in some measure contribute to our experience of self-alienation. Have we become caught up in the frenzy, the competitiveness, and the meaninglessness of our times? Is our lifestyle hooked into endless distractions? The evidence of this is found in one's experience of feeling out-of-control, exhausted, lethargic, bored.

In the end, whatever our understanding of what-went-wrong, we should not assign blame for our unlived lives to outside circumstances or social conditioning. However prone we are to justifying our personal dysfunction – explaining our behaviors, re-enforcing negative beliefs, rationalizing our mistakes

– the narrative we tell about what-went-wrong freezes self-understanding and robs us of freedom.

When we stay in the *victim position* and plead helpless to the force of outer circumstance, our power of self-determination is lost. But our personal power can be reclaimed if we follow the path of a victor and let go of our victim narratives. On the other side of justified powerlessness, the stories our lives want to write begin to move in brand new directions.

It takes courage to examine our self-defeating patterns of thinking and behaving, and to acknowledge the negative consequences that follow our wrong choices. Living is about learning, and learning involves making many mistakes. When we run away from our personal failures, we miss the opportunity to see what was missing in our consciousness that created negative outcomes. Transcending negative self-reproach, the art of self-forgiveness lies in the gentle correction of the mistakes we make.

deep change

Pure tragedy, most would agree, occurs when the story of one's life goes unrecognized – even more tragic when the story is recognized, but refused. At every turn, we are invited to make a leap into the unknown – living the questions that help us find our true purpose and realize our hidden potential. Our grasp of true being emerges with each right insight and each meaningful action.

Alienation begins where there is resistance to wakefulness and a disregard for value. The moral choices we make define our lives for better or for worse. Seven expressions of alienation are laziness, anger, greed, pride, lust, envy, and excess. Negative emotions arise as the ego puts forward its agenda of craving pleasure, averting pain, and having its own way. Essentially, moral performance falters where there is a disregard both of self and of the needs of others.

We remain adrift as long as we fail to address the root causes of our suffering. It is often argued that we have no time to heal. And so we run around, but we continue to suffer – and to afflict suffering on one another. More attention often gets placed on looking for the relief of symptoms than on finding the root causes and true resolve of our afflictions. But the symptoms only recur, and escalate.

The task of awareness calls forth practices of attention and intention. As consciousness and commitment evolve, the ego is unmasked and loses its power, and one's orientation to meaning and value comes more to the fore. This brings about a loosening of attachment to materialistic goals, together with a new determination to change in the way that one can.

I recall Barkley kicking off one of our conversations with the opening statement: "Man, I have to grow up once again!" He was clearly alluding to the truth that self-development is a non-stop process. Continuing his self-expression: "What a horrible feeling you have when you find out how little you know. You thought you had a handle on things, something happens, and then you realize that you are no further ahead than before."

I suggested that we all get discouraged when caught in these psychic undertows that pull us down, and sometimes tear us apart. He frowned, "That's hard to hear. I like to think I am in control," then added, "But when I feel humbled, it helps. I am not all I think I am. I am really starting to recognize I have a long way to go. I have a lot to learn."

Certainly, one's ability to find solutions to human problems emerges through the skillful practice of awareness. As intention strengthens, and marries one's expanding awareness, the web of error begins to dissolve. Each leap of wisdom creates a new experience of freedom and bliss – arising as we find truth, awaken beauty, and realize love.

Barkley made an optimistic last pitch for change: "Growth has to happen now, not tomorrow! How can I change if I keep doing everything the same without creating space and time in my life to manage change? I need to plan to succeed, rather than setting myself up for staying stuck in the same patterns."

"I like to think I am in control. But when I feel humbled, it helps. I am not all I think I am. I am really starting to recognize I have a long way to go. I have a lot to learn."

10. Wisdom in Action

You can change the next moment;
you can do something different, something enlightened;
something creative, imaginative, and fresh;
something compassionate and wise.

Lama Surya Das

Our desire to know and our achievement of knowledge is not
an end point. There is more. Our knowing is oriented to
action; we desire to know, because we desire to act, and act
intelligently. Our experiencing, understanding, and judging
are directed not to just what is, but what is to be done,
not just to know reality, but creating reality,
and creating ourselves in the process.

Walter Conn

Your beliefs become your thoughts,
your thoughts become your words,
your words become your actions,
your actions become your habits,
your habits become your values,
your values become your destiny.

Mahatma Gandhi

being right

"I was what you would call a pretty stubborn individual. Once my mind was made up, that was that. I was very sure about myself, and about being right. Actually, I was in disbelief when others had an opinion different from my own. Why doesn't this person realize I am right?"

A mutual friend put me in touch with Pete, and in a first telephone conversation, Pete shared: "I have a passion for personal development." That cemented our friendship, and here, in one of our many conversations, Pete describes an experience of unmasking pride, and turning his stubborn need to be right into an enlarged openness of heart.

Pete Lavoie

As Pete tells it: "This never-being-wrong led to many emotional blow-ups. I would react in two ways: explosion or implosion. I would have an extreme reaction, a big emotional outburst, or I would put a cap on my feelings that made me feel that I was damaging my insides. Often, I would abandon relationships. This emotional roller-coaster eventually made me realize that I was completely off-centre."

I encouraged Pete to say more. "The cost was huge – in fact, I had two long-term romantic relationships and one long-time friendship fall apart. I began to wonder why this was happening. Others seemed so much happier. Why weren't my friendships fulfilling? There had to be a common thread, something that would explain this pattern of dysfunction. In the end, I saw that I was the problem! Then I began to ask myself what I really wanted in my relationships, and what I could do differently."

"Some new insights began to brew. What struck me was that I ought to give people what I myself longed for – to be supported, listened to, acclaimed, loved. I never felt that I was getting enough attention myself. Things really changed when it hit me that my friends had the exact same needs as me. Could I offer support to my friends? I put new energy into listening to and encouraging them – aware how much I would value the reciprocation of the same attention. Also, I really began to work on my patience."

As Pete's passion turned into compassion, his story began to take a happy turn: "This pivotal insight brought me to a whole new pattern of interaction with others. I let myself be guided by the rule of thumb that if you want to be listened to, listen to others. And if you want to be acknowledged, acknowledge others. It became very clear to me that the way to get is to give – and give it first, give relentlessly."

Pete continued: "I started to notice that what came back to me was more than what I had given out. My emotional habits underwent change. I was no longer only rooting for myself, and no longer convinced that my opinion was always right. I was much less reactive. In fact, I actually developed a great curiosity to hear ideas other than my own. Indeed, asking questions is far more effective than giving answers. All this had the impact of improving my self-confidence, and I was able to process big emotions without blowing my top, or gluing my top down until it exploded."

The moral of the story, mused Pete, is that "When you become clear about your intention – in my case, this was related to the dynamics of friendship – your actions become wise in regard to that agency. By agency, I mean what are you invested in? What are you dedicated to? By acting in reference to wise intention, you understand what needs to happen. You become committed to your values and intentions."

"I could have stayed in my emotional powerlessness, but I chose to act in a new way. I chose to examine my way of relating to others, and to embrace change. Today, more than anything, what makes me feel somewhat wiser is the realization that I am actually quite a beginner in everything. This attitude fills me with wonder, and makes me excited about the adventure of every relationship."

Pete's transformative experience seems to have resulted from three key factors of self-development: keen attention, critical reflection, and committed intention. Authenticity, as we have described it, develops in the conjunction of experiencing, asking questions, seeking correct self-understanding, choosing value, and acting towards meaning. For Pete, all these components were integral to a growth in self-knowledge that enabled him to attain a new quality of interpersonal relationship.

daring the deed

Awareness is the empowerment of action. As Pete's story reveals, mindful attention and self-enquiry underpin our capacity for right action. We are challenged to live the answers that are born from asking the right questions and cultivating wise insight. In the different stages of emergent consciousness, habits of attention and intention find deep congruence.

Why do we so often act against our better judgment? Even though we recognize something to be of worth, why do we in fact settle for something worse? What sense can we make of refusing what is in our best interests? Certainly, our failure to choose intelligently is based upon a preference for short-lived satisfactions versus genuine value. Our egoism readily avoids hard choices, opting instead for immediate gratification in place of long-term benefit.

Only when we answer to our desire for the true good, both for oneself and others, do we evade the pleasure trap and evoke what is truly worthwhile. Then it is easy to see that the beauty of an action is found in the purity of intention that guides it. Indeed, genuine happiness requires both insight and courage – seeking and abiding in the truth that sets us free. We have to both discern and choose the good.

History teaches us that adherence to truth leads to great action. When we live out of refined insight, we learn to trust our choices - to trust them precisely because in them we find a congruence of wisdom, compassion, and respect. Indeed, it is our deeds that make us who we are.

Authenticity always asks us to play for high stakes, and this entails a total commitment to discovering our wholeness. Either we are seeking our true purpose, or simply drifting along. If we remain indecisive and just go with the flow, we forfeit finding a meaningful path. On the other hand, if we surrender to what our life tells us it wants, we embark on a journey that will carry us from indetermination to intentionality, from ignorance to insight, and from worry to wisdom.

Seeking a freedom we do not yet know, many different practices of attention and intention contribute to the emergence of authenticity. There is always further to go – the process is ongoing, always shifting, ever-developing. As we observe our experience, question it, test our understanding of it, and act with meaningful intention, we lay the cornerstone upon which genuine human happiness is progressively realized.

proactive transformation

It is said that each person has a story – a set of challenging circumstances to face, a road of trials to travel, a particular burden of darkness to bear. Here the question arises: to what extent are our lives defined from the outside, by the force of circumstance and the determinations of nature?

Many argue for their limitations, and find themselves stuck in a victim position and powerless to shape the story of their lives. This creates a good breeding ground for resentment and hopelessness. But others, even in the face of huge obstacles, seem to be able to break through their limits, and realize the impossible.

What does it mean to live proactively, and not passively? Is it true that one's capacity to imagine new possibility rests more on derived meaning than on the notion that our lives are determined by conditions and conditioning? If so, how do we learn to move from reaction to intentional action?

One answer to the question of *fate* is summed up in the view that though we are conditioned, we are not determined. Each of us grows up in a particular context – historical, cultural, familial, genetic – that defines a range of bounded possibility. On the other hand, however, there lies within each of us a *force of becoming* that invites us into a world of boundless opportunity.

The call I heard, at the age of 22, to make my life an adventure of love, gave me a clear direction of meaning and a new confidence of being. Rather than being defeated by personal limitations, I embraced them as a summons to learn. From then on, I came to know that the story of my life would be shaped by the choices I made; and that by acting with strength of purpose, I would find my true self.

In the context of our modern world, there seems to be a growing disenchantment that gives way to deep cynicism, powerlessness, and widespread complacency. The fatal allurements of consumerism support the fantasy that increased material abundance brings full happiness. Furthermore, technological advances have inflated our sense of power, thus creating a false notion of progress. So too, alienation from the natural world is plunging us into a deep ecological crisis. These dark times invite extraordinary new consciousness, creativity, and courage to meet the difficult challenges we face – they call us to act with heroic determination.

A favourite aphorism of mine: it is easier to light a candle than curse the darkness. In search of new light, the task of history looks to discern what wants to emerge, and by re-imagining new possibilities, we become open to the miracles of human potential. The many challenges we meet help us awaken a new sense of belonging to life and to each other, and to find a new depth of human freedom.

sustainable authenticity

When discussing the dynamics of human authenticity, I often introduce the metaphor of *driving a car*, and invite everyone to reflect on what makes a good driver *good*. As we identify the different qualities that enable a driver to perform well, they always seems to boil down to three key operations: attentiveness, sound judgment, and decisiveness.

Attentiveness consists in being focused – a function of not being distracted, or emotionally off-balance, or in too much of a hurry. You must be continuously in tune with everything that is going on around you at all times. Eyes do most of the work, and ears are important too. Of course, making good use of your mirrors (three are better than two, or one) is all-important. The more you see, the better your performance.

Sound judgment consists in interpreting the incoming data (traffic configurations, road conditions), and discerning how to put yourself into a relationship with all the other cars on the road (including defensive driving to protect yourself from other drivers whose performance is lacking). You are required to continually make judgments about the choices being made from moment-to-moment: slowing down, speeding up, changing lanes, signaling, passing others.

Often this is a split-second process. Decisiveness consists in acting with determination, or reacting without hesitation, in response to the steady flow of data pouring in during this fast-moving drama.

There is absolutely no time off, because the configuration of the traffic is constantly changing, and so the operations of being attentive, exercising judgment, and making decisions are non-stop – and often happening simultaneously. Even as you slip into the right-hand lane, you will observe a whole new arrangement of vehicles, and be compelled to make newer judgments and newer decisions.

This can be brought to a whole other level by examining your own driving performance over and above the external traffic dynamics that are in play. This means evaluating your own competence in the exercise of attentiveness, making judgments, and decision-making. What is enhancing or subtracting from the quality of your performance? Here we are talking about a driver's physical and emotional processes as much as about traffic configurations. In truth, it is your awareness that is doing the driving.

The attention we pay to growth in awareness gives energetic momentum to the unfolding of our lives. Not only do we bring awareness to the full range of our experience, but also, we need to be *aware of our awareness*, evaluating our performance in terms of cultivating a quality of steady attentiveness, deep understanding, and prudent action. In life, it is the awareness we have that *drives* our unfolding story.

Faithfulness to the task of transformation moves us out of powerlessness. We make ourselves who we are by acting upon our knowledge of the good. As we have seen, there are successive steps in one's development: exacting self-observation, careful interpretation, moral courage, decisive action. Over time, self-knowledge accrues as a function of a practiced attention to personal experience, along with a discipline of keen discernment. Right choices follow closely on the heels of insight and wise intention. If we find the right questions, right insight will follow.

Each of us is the agent of our own authenticity – needing to jump into a dynamic process of actualizing the truth of who we are and who we are to become. To find a sound direction of meaning, each of us is compelled to listen to the inner call that points the way to our true path. The way of sustainable authenticity suggests that there can be no end to our efforts to reinvent what it means to be human.

In the course of my conversation with Pete, he emphasized the link between authenticity and value-based intention: "It is when we take a look at the nature of our suffering that we begin to understand why our actions are often unwise. Right action is that which sets us free – it is defined in terms of your goal.

The key to understanding right action is to sincerely ask yourself what is important to you. What do you live for?"

"Today, more than anything, what makes me feel somewhat wiser is the realization that I am actually quite a beginner in everything."

11. Self-Affirmation

*…when I love, I sense, with an altogether new intensity,
that I am. To love is to feel in oneself
the current that flows out of the heart of all existence.*
Sebastian Moore

*Our busyness is often a distraction, a way of avoiding others,
avoiding intimacy, avoiding ourselves.
We keep busy to push back our fears, our loneliness,
our self-doubt, our questions about purposes and ends.*
Philip Simmons

*Loving yourself…does not mean being self-absorbed;
it means welcoming yourself as the most honored guest
in your own heart.*
Margo Anand

inner befriending

"At a *Friendship Inside Out* circle," recounted Leyla, "my curiosity became sharply focused on the theme of *inner friendship*. I was drawn to that retreat by an already-existing desire to attain deeper levels of connection and fulfilment with friends. What emerged and was nurtured in that circle experience was what I call the golden key of self-befriending."

Leyla continued: "It became apparent to me that my relationships with others were a reflection of my relationship with myself, and in fact, mirrored some of my own inner challenges. Sometimes, I had difficulty opening up to others, and this was a function of not trusting myself and running away from the parts of myself that involved shame and pain. In my youth I experienced a lot of isolation and loneliness. I was longing for a meaningful, nourishing connection. But as much as I needed to be seen, heard, and valued by others, I wasn't exposed to people who could truly receive me, and so it didn't feel safe to open up."

Leyla Demir

In conversation with Leyla, it became all the more clear to me that personal alienation begins in one's estrangement from self-love and expresses itself in different forms of self-abandonment. And so in the neglect of our bodies, the denial of emotions, and the disregard of spiritual values, we become strangers to ourselves. This avoidance of self blocks the affirmation of personal experience in both its positive and negative aspects, and thus we lose access to our integral potential.

The key question for me was: how do we come to truly believe in ourselves? Or, otherwise stated, how do we affirm the lives we truly want to live? In response to these questions, Leyla zeroed in on the theme of inner authenticity: "The main thing for me was facing my vulnerabilities. I had to come to terms with my own humanity. Allowing what is – my feelings, my thoughts, my experiences – to be, without judgement from myself. To receive them with gentleness, compassion, and curiosity. To listen to what fundamental needs lie within these experiences."

Leyla paused, before adding: "I feel as though we forget what it is to be human beings. We hide our weaknesses in an attempt to be impressive or lovable, ignoring the fact that our fears, pain, and personal challenges are just as much part of being alive. We are pushed to show strength and competence, and so we put on masks of invincibility."

A breakthrough experience for Leyla came with recognizing "…the importance of being and living in wholeness. It was in witnessing and accepting those parts of myself that I had been rejecting on some level

– the tough parts that were damaged, struggling, or unaccomplished – which brought about a greater sense of completeness and fullness of self. Ironically, it was through loving the weak aspects of myself that I actually felt my true strength."

Adding to Leyla's insight, I commented that this *being human*, once awakened and embraced, draws forth a new depth of happiness that can be shared with others. Through befriending both the bright and dark aspects of ourselves, we integrate the different sides of who we are, and certainly such affirmation of self is integral to one's individual journey to wholeness, as well as the health of one's interpersonal encounters.

Leyla describes this in her own experience: "I ended up becoming a good listener at a young age partly because of my innate sense of how important it is to share and be received by others. I was offering outwardly what I was needing inwardly. My attention to other persons enabled me to acknowledge the vulnerable parts of myself that longed for deep acceptance. As I learned to befriend more and more of my total being, I experienced greater integrity within myself. In turn, growth in inner acceptance taught me to affirm others, and to be present to them from a place of realness, strength, and honesty."

self-love as self-gift

As we bring forth a quality of attention and intention, we find an inner connection that allows us to come home to the life we are meant to live. This provides the basis for the fulfilment of our core human longing: the desire to belong to oneself and to others, as well as to the natural world.

Ultimately, the goal of inward self-encounter is to shine light on how one is to live a genuine life. Self-attention, when it is not ego-driven, connects us to our essential nature and translates into self-love. Each individual discovers a specialness – a singular quality of being, unique gifts, a hidden purpose that calls forth the task of developing our creative potential. The tragedy of life is not to recognize that something special about oneself.

Self-alienation, monk and author Sebastian Moore suggests, results from a radical distrust of our basic goodness. When we are out of touch with our essential nature, we see ourselves in a very limited way. We doubt our potential, or deny it, and build personal identity around powerlessness and pathology. Disconnection from self-love feeds the distrust of our ability to be a source of happiness for others.

To reclaim our true worth is to fashion a vision whose foundation is rooted in our original goodness. The trust of our intrinsic goodness activates a force of character and power of intelligence that puts us onto a path of self-reliance. Self-trust is the cornerstone of growth, and trumps any self-devaluation, self-rejection, or shame. The goodness we affirm organizes itself in our intentions, expresses itself in our actions, and wins us the freedom for which we long.

As I learn to trust the deep yearnings of my heart, the confidence I have in the unique promise of my life grows stronger. This self-trust empowers me to embrace the challenges which that promise invites. Truly, when I am able to affirm *something special* about myself, I can make my life a gift to others. Motivated by a desire to share who I am, I learn to trust that my specialness can be enjoyed by others. As Moore highlights: I want my life to be for another, or others – in this way my life finds its greatest fulfillment.

Certainly, as we value ourselves, we ignite a hidden power of love that translates into a deep respect of self, and everyone. Self-discipline and self-control flow out of a vision of being that is in tune with our individual specialness, and with the way in which one's intrinsic goodness wants to manifest. Opportunities intersect with our deepest intentions to lead us along a path of meaningful self-giving.

A question that often arises is in regard to the difference between self-nurture and self-absorption, between vital self-awareness and what some refer to as navel-gazing? Selfishness, which is a turning in on self, is synonymous with unhappiness – it is born in fear and endlessly seeks out its own protection. When one thinks only of oneself, one's life spins on vanity. Such self-obsession leads to a lack of confidence that fuels a thirst for power over others. Because the ego does not like vulnerability, it tries to override insecurity with excessive ambition, aggressive money-making, possessive relationships, addictive behaviors, self-destructive lifestyles, and the like. The ego goes into overdrive as it tries to compensate for gaps in self-love.

Self-nurture is, in fact, the very opposite of egoism. The care of self is the very foundation that supports one's capacity to love outwardly. By definition, love can only be given away – it cannot be kept for itself. By *being for others* we affirm the truth of who we are. Thus, true self-love is synonymous with self-giving.

identity inside out

The task of shaping authentic identity is never easy and never final. It is a tall challenge to live in deep obedience to the wisdom and values that frame personal integrity. Through ongoing self-discovery, we activate a power of inner determination that progressively allows us to choose the life we want to live.

On the other hand, dead identity is when we stop becoming who we are. It is living according to cultural norms, social conformity, peer pressure, the ego's drive to perform. Our lives become defined from the outside in. Lacking inner drive and direction, we forfeit our individual creativity, and become victims of the trend of depersonalization in mass society – less and less different from each other, yet increasingly isolated and lonely.

To define ourselves from the inside out is daunting in an age where we are under the influence of mass culture and mass communication. Am I thinking and choosing what everybody else is thinking and choosing? Am I swayed more by promptings coming from the external world than from inner purpose? Do I give myself permission to live the life that is right for me – in accord with the truth of who I am?

The quest for inner belonging compels us to engage ourselves at a deeper level and nurture the seeds of individual creativity hidden inside ourselves. As one comes to affirm the authentic purpose of one's life, the artificial agenda of the ego is laid aside, allowing us to find a genuine self-image that reflects the unique meaning of one's life.

Personal identity evolves out of the questions that we continue to ask about who we are, where we belong, what matters most to us, and what are our deepest values and meanings. It is never fixed. Any identity or image of self is only a resting place – we need to continuously let go of whom we think we are in order to jump into an adventure of unending self-discovery.

self-intimacy

Certainly, the way of distraction marks out a path of self-alienation. A lack of inwardness inhibits one's ability to come into an intimate encounter with self. If our attention is turned to the external world most of the time, and scattered in a thousand different directions, we lose touch with our own inner experience, and thus abandon our transformative potential.

The way of attention, on the other hand, builds a momentum of personal growth. Through ongoing experiences of self-presence, self-understanding, and self-actualization, we are able to attain a depth of inner freedom that translates into true happiness. As we move beyond fragmentation, we discover the deep ground of authentic being.

Self-intimacy gives us contact with the unconscious – new worlds of meaning are slowly introduced to consciousness through images arising from within the depths of the psyche. These symbolic images lie beyond rational control, beyond what the ego can comprehend. They are voices of the essential self – symbols of authenticity that reveal to us our undiscovered selves. And, as Leyla has suggested, a quality of inner connection enables a quality of outer connection: indeed, self-intimacy draws forth our capacity to be intimate with others.

Stillness creates space for self-observation, wise insight, and sound judgment. As we cultivate still and alert attention, we are able to listen to our bodies and witness our restless psychic processes. Through observing our conditioned thoughts and emotions as they arise, we free ourselves from the grip of reactive behaviours. A habit of stillness allows us to be completely available to experience – awake, engaged, alert, and unhurried.

Inner befriending sets forth an agenda of self-nurture – time for inner healing, for rest, for play, for renewal, for deep listening. We always seem to be fighting time, or running out of it. Do we create enough *slow time* to become attuned to the timeless dimensions of life? Still water runs deep – in the experience of silence, we enter into a new stream of awareness, inspired by images that reveal hidden dimensions of self and meaning. Without silence, these images are lost to consciousness, and thereby they narrow down our range of future possibility.

Different practices of meditation direct the mind to depth, and teach the heart to open. Because the psyche is an unstable state of consciousness, we need to find a stable centre. Penetrating deeper, beyond the turbulence one finds in the surface mind, we find a more restful calm – we develop an inner trust of self that allows us to tap into the deeper source of energy where one's real life goes on.

A rhythm of *activity* and *withdrawal from activity* in one's day-to-day experience lets us come to know ourselves better. It is the same as eating and getting hungry, exerting self and resting, getting involved with people and withdrawing from the crowd. In the habit of returning to self, one is able to source new energy and self-love, and to affirm others more deeply.

This is reflected in Leyla's practice of self-presence at the end of each day. As she describes it: "I sit quietly with myself, and gently enter into a process that lets me listen to my inner world with genuine care. By giving space for my feelings in their full range, I open into what wants to be heard, and trust that whatever emerges is part of me and deserves respect."

Leyla took a long breath, and then concluded: "Afterwards, I write down everything that is revealed, and then try to identify the true needs suggested within my feelings. This practice of personal befriending is a daily gift to myself that enables me to be available to my experience as an inner witness and compassionate companion. It is an ever-evolving blessing that continuously draws forth new depths of self-awareness and self-love."

"Allowing what is – my feelings, my thoughts, my experiences – to be, without judgement from myself. To receive them with gentleness, compassion, and curiosity. To listen to what fundamental needs lie within these experiences."

12. Quantum Friendship

I am because you are.
Ubuntu wisdom

*Empathic listening gets inside another person's frame of reference. You look out through it, you see the world the way they see the world, you understand their paradigm, you understand how they feel ...
you're listening to understand.
You're focused on receiving the deep communication of another human soul.*
Stephen Covey

*Each friend represents a world in us,
a world not born until they arrive,
and it is only by this meeting that
a new world is born.*
Anaïs Nin

friendship inside out

My gratitude for the friends who have gifted my life over the years lies beyond the reach of words. Each friend showed up, it seems, at just the right time! Like me, do you sometimes wonder how friends find each other? Do we seek one another out

Solomon Krueger

long before our paths coincide? Is the intersection of our lives the play of destiny, and part of a larger pattern of meaning? My own sense is that the poetry of friendship ignites inside a dynamic framework of attraction and meaning – that, in the end, might best be described as a mysterious force of love.

One friend who showed up in my life is Solomon. We discovered a strong resonance on our first encounter, then teamed up to co-facilitate a series of vision quests and friendship circles. "The promise of every friendship," Solomon says, "is found in the unique gifts unfolding inside each friend. The conversation and intimacy that one shares with a particular friend will not be found with anyone else – this makes our encounters in each moment that much more significant and precious."

Friendships, as Solomon highlights, are truly one-of-a-kind – each giving expression to unique creativity and delight. Each relationship walks a singular path marked by particular challenges and tasks of growth. Friends trade affection, gratitude, respect, wisdom and loving kindness that find expression in a wide diversity of interactions. Carried along in the mysterious unfolding of new moments in time, every further encounter reveals more of each friend to the other.

Solomon and Dominic met over 18 years ago, and have been close friends ever since. "The two of us," describes Solomon, "mirror back to one another a passion for authenticity, along with a permission to enjoy life to its fullest. In this manner, we encourage and validate common ideals in each other." He adds appreciatively: "I was aware that I was in this experience of friendship, and that it was very nourishing."

"As our friendship deepened over the years," Solomon continued, "Dominic could understand what I was experiencing – he was someone who could really *get* me. We have always had a great readiness to go deeper. In each interaction, we noticed things we hadn't noticed before, we felt things we hadn't felt before. Each encounter was the seed of the next. It seemed that our friendship just kept getting better all the time."

Highlighting the great value he places on the gift of mutual witnessing that friends bestow on each other, Solomon added: "We have shared hard times, and our struggles have been a mirror to one another. Dominic can challenge me. He can ask questions that go right to the heart of the matter. He can see through my self-deception and point out my blind spots. He has certainly helped me unmask my ego."

"How special it is to be seen and heard by another, and through a heart-felt bond realize that we are not so separate or alone, or even different." In an appreciation that runs deep for his friend of 18 years, Solomon concluded: "I am very grateful that I will never be completely lost, or ever in total darkness, because Dominic is always there, helping me to remember who I am!"

to be for another

Friends work out a way of being together in different interactive patterns: play and recreation, sexual intimacy, artistic collaboration, intellectual creativity, parenting, athletic teamwork, professional life, community action, and spiritual solidarity. In these varied interplays of friendship, our life biographies progressively unfold their hidden stories of meaning.

Friends collaborate in seeking truth, doing justice, and searching for personal fulfilment. Together we make love, learn, toil, co-create, play and pray. In good times, we celebrate awareness and self-discovery, and the joy of authentic being. In dark times, we bear one another's burdens, finding an increase of courage through compassionate embrace. At all times, human intimacy calls forth our individual capacities for creativity and love, and allows us to know the mutual delight of deep belonging.

The notion of *interdependence* points to the essence of a healthy relationship – it supports both differentiation and communion. To be different is to honour oneself as original – to affirm one's subjective meanings, unique expression, and individual creativity. But happiness is never a solitary achievement. Two persons, in a communion of mutual presence, create a dance of bliss – friends simply enjoy themselves enjoying each other. Deep affection, trust, empathy, honesty, gentleness and generosity are born through encounter.

Think of a seed that holds the mystery of what it will become, yet needs fertile soil, along with the right amount of moisture and sunshine, in order to grow in an optimal way. One of the richest blessings that friends bestow on one another is an expression of deep acceptance – this is the soil in which we grow best. Talents and treasures buried within ourselves are sometimes not even imagined until they come into recognition through an experience of being deeply loved by another.

Like a seed that finds fertile soil, our latent potential germinates when planted in a field of nourishing friendship. We, too, exist as a milieu for others – and the best gift we bring to friends is the enlargement of our own consciousness and love, to serve as nurturance for their growth. Thus we play an essential role in one another's continuous evolution.

Every new relationship dares me to grow, to let more aliveness into my life. In the never-ending theatre of self-discovery, I am always in some sort of dialogue with myself. As I befriend another, I allow my self-awareness to interface with someone who is a stranger to myself. In this way, I open myself to a greater depth of self-knowledge. Authentic friendship is never static – it is always on the move reaching towards a hidden richness of meaning.

In my experience of friendship, I have found that one plus one adds up to more than the sum of its parts, and gives birth to an amazing amplification of energy within each individual. But, in the refusal of authenticity, when we go it alone, we become isolated and lonely. In ego-driven interactions, one plus one adds up to zero, or even less!

When all else has been said, the true difference in human relationship is choosing to *be there* for one another. In the loyal back and forth of loving kindness, we enter new worlds of belonging, and are ever reminded that love contains infinite possibilities. It is when we learn to let go of the separate self and surrender to love that we find the courage to do together what is difficult to do alone.

Something that I learned early on in life: friendship is reaped because it is sown and cultivated. The best way to *get* friends is to *pour out* friendship. There is always the risk of becoming jaded by experiences of unreciprocated friendship and betrayal. Certainly, love is not always returned by those to whom it is given, but it does come back from the universe a hundredfold – at least, it always has in my experience.

entanglement

I speak of *quantum friendship* in order to highlight the profound nature of our participation in one another's lives. More than journeying alongside each other, through ongoing interaction and depth encounter, we take part in the mystery of each other's becoming. As we have been discussing, friendships introduce us to our hidden possibilities, and enable us to uncover completely new dimensions of self. Each interaction both alters the other, and at the same time expands our self-intimacy.

Truly, we thrive in relationship. Friendships are born in the mystery of attraction, in the confluence of meaning, and in the gratuitousness of destiny. Our lives are profoundly relational, and those with whom our life adventure coincides help create and strengthen a synergy of passion and purpose.

In quantum theory, the term *entanglement* refers to the mysterious co-relation between particles, which, once they get involved with each other, create waves that exist in a unified field. Likewise, in the domain of friendship, once you interact, you become entangled – hearts and minds become part of an interconnected whole; communicate with each other in mysterious ways/waves, and cannot be described independently.

Quantum waves move instantly over a distance, even when separated with no direct communication. So too, friends impact one another's lives even at a distance – one changes and the other changes simultaneously. Not boxed into a specific location, friends are everywhere, at the same time! A case in point, Solomon and Dominic have for years lived many thousand miles apart from each other.

The boundless dimension of friendship brings us into an expanded vision of reality whereby we recognize our essential unity beyond a consciousness of separateness and beyond the conflicts that inevitably arise. We see the other in oneself, and the self in the other – so we speak of friends as being on the same wave length. There is a sense of having the special connection, and behaving as one.

Quantum theory suggests that much more is going on with respect to the reality of relationship than what we understand. The exchange of our lives with one another creates an amplification of consciousness that introduces us to infinite possibilities. The unity of love that we experience in any journey of authentic friendship creates the ongoing miracle that leads us out of ignorance and illusion and isolation.

interplayfulness

In our friendship circles, Solomon invites participants to choose several attributes of friendship that stand out in their own experience. This opens up a wide range of themes – my own choice of emphasis being *empathy*, *awareness*, and *playfulness*.

A friend's empathetic presence is a gift that lifts us outside time and space. When seen and felt by another, I no longer feel alone. The sacredness of relationship is realized in the experience of having a companion to my joy and my sorrow – my happiness when shared with another is amplified, while my suffering when shared is diminished. A good friend is attentive, loyal, available – right there with you, through thick and thin.

Empathy and finesse in communication seem to walk hand in hand. Through genuine self-expression and deep listening, we connect – we create a dance of dialogue that enables friends to get inside each other's frame of reference. The discovery of self is not realized on one's own, but born in the communication of experience, insight, and meaning with others.

Reciprocal self-discovery is sparked through this interface of awareness. A shared practice of authenticity between friends supports a mutual evolution of consciousness – I make known to friends what I am discovering about myself, and they, in like manner, share the story of their unfolding experience and insight.

It is not always easy to open up to others. Relatedness is demanding because it confronts the unknown, and our fear of it. As we speak truth and listen with sensitivity to one another, relationships of trust are formed that enable us to befriend the darker parts of ourselves. Often, in the mud of our imperfection, it is the acceptance and gentle correction of friends that allows us to forgive the mistakes of our past and learn to trust the goodness we have yet to bring forth.

Of course, it is not always easy to be with ourselves – but without a strong inner connection, we cannot have vibrant outer connections. Taking time for inwardness, we open up to the truth of our experience, both light and dark. The cultivation of self-intimacy provides a basis for growth in self-knowledge that empowers our ability to have intimate contact with others.

Adding to what has been said, I think that *playfulness* lies at the heart of human connection. To play is to be at ease, to have fun, to trust, to laugh, and to know joy. Like children immersed in a spontaneous delight of each unfolding moment, we awaken the freedom to be who we are. Play is a great antidote to stress, conflict, and affliction.

Solomon puts it very nicely: "Playfulness is a beautiful aspect of dialogue with oneself or others. There's an anticipation of listening, of curiosity, and of discovery of what will come – which ultimately brings new ideas, a synthesis, and satisfaction. There is also a sense of freedom in this space to improvise, imagine, explore, and experiment for its own sake!" Solomon tags on another thought: "Friendship is at its best when it just happens – with openness, trust, and deep listening."

Dominic had a similar drift when speaking about his long-time friendship with Solomon: "The centerpiece for me in our spiritual friendship is laughter. It is an ability to laugh at ourselves and at the crazy situations we find ourselves in that defines our connection to each other, and our relationship to life itself. Life is about play, about having fun, about creating, about experiencing and growing; these are important shared values that have never had to be articulated, but have been simply understood in the way that we are."

The energy of friendship comes from a deep source – soulful connection, true belonging, a pure heart, generosity of spirit. I am inspired by the five words: "I am because you are!" They form one translation of *ubuntu* – an African tradition of reciprocal human goodness and respect, highlighting that individual personhood rests on the quality of love received from a community, including ancestral spirits. Truly, the embodied, intelligent, and heart-to-heart friendship that has nurtured me on my life journey has allowed me to become who I am – my heart is filled with gratitude as I write.

"Playfulness is a beautiful aspect of dialogue with oneself or others. There's an anticipation of listening, of curiosity, and of discovery of what will come – which ultimately brings new ideas, a synthesis, and satisfaction. There is also a sense of freedom in this space to improvise, imagine, explore, and experiment for its own sake!"

13. INTERDEPENDENCE

The universe is a continuous web.
Touch it at any point and the whole web quivers.
Stanley Kunitz

Differences among people are the seeds of creation,
sparking the continuous process
of innovation and evolution.
Mary Parker Follet

The central demand is to surrender our exclusivity:
everything that defines us as against each other.
Joseph Campbell

web of relationship

I recall the warm friendly smile that greeted me some years ago, along with the introduction "My name is Jihad". Immediately, I was drawn to the aura of kindness that emanated from the stranger standing in front of me. Jihad tells me that new acquaintances often feel a little awkward when meeting him for the first time – some even ask, "How can a guy like you be named Jihad?"

Jihad points out that in the non-Muslim world most translate *jihad* to mean holy war, conquest, and violence. But he puts a somewhat different spin on what his name means: "*Jihad* is an Arabic word that comes from the root *jihada* – to exert effort. The meaning of *true jihad* is striving to be genuine in everything that you do."

Jihad Hyjazie

"My name symbolizes putting forth my best effort to achieve beauty and justice, both inwardly and outwardly. There is good and evil, light and darkness that I cannot ignore by simply putting my head in the sand," Jihad continues. "True jihad ultimately means becoming a warrior of peace. Equipped with generosity, kindness, forgiveness, and education, I stand for the oppressed and try to promote a better future. My jihad is to push back evil and overcome injustice with goodness. This is how both the oppressed and the oppressors can truly be set free."

From that first encounter onwards, Jihad and I have felt a deep kinship of spirit. His passion for justice, his unreserved goodness, and his nonjudgmental embrace of everyone are the strong cornerstones of his authenticity. Jihad's driving intent is to give expression to love through reflection and action. In his own words: "Every time I see or touch the humanity of another, I experience an intensity of feeling. Love is the steady adrenaline that drives me, gives me courage and a sense of purpose – it is self-generating. Life becomes a real nightmare when love is absent."

Jihad optimistically suggests that a cross-cultural convergence is gaining new momentum amongst those who share a unity of intention: "In every place on the planet, people are moving towards universal human values. No matter where you come from, no matter what your background, there is a collective movement to affirm a certain set of truths that bring individuals peace, beauty, and fulfillment. Since we are all the same, it will bring peace for all."

I asked Jihad how this experience of *interconnection* is being realized. "It is heard in our stories," he replied. "We are finding each other, and coming together, and uniting. The *oneness* we seek lives inside our hearts: inside me, and inside you and your story. We are experiencing interconnection. Genuine individuals find each other along the road, and powerful transformative encounters are taking place. Those who are listening to the truth are converging – as we come to know each other, we will join together to progressively create a global manifestation of truth."

a new global reality

Some time ago, Jihad invited me to speak to Muslim students at Concordia University in Montreal. I began by describing how the notion of a *global village* became real for me when, as a young adult, I set forth on a two-year adventure around the planet. Leaving my bounded cultural milieu, I struck out into the big, wide world with impassioned wonder. Though quite timid, I was eager to explore the vast unknown – before long, I knew that the adventure of my life was underway.

So much to breathe in! There was an abundance of natural beauty: ocean sunrises, arid desert landscapes, lush rainforests, pulsing rivers, mountain-top splendours. But also, I witnessed so much suffering: teeming over-population, urban squalor, the drama of ego desire, extensive pollution, crime and corruption, human toil, intolerable poverty, hungry children, war and violence. What also made an impression upon me was the abundance of spiritual passion everywhere to be found: fervent religious rituals, mystical imagination, sacred dance, heroic compassion and generosity, visionary fire, blissful friendship, the joy of love.

As I journeyed across the face of the Earth, I felt lost in the multitudes and, most of the time, quite overwhelmed by the immensity of beauty and suffering that I witnessed. This evoked in me a desire to contribute in some way to the common good – the making of the global village – though I had no idea of what role I could play.

Thrown in, as it were, to the diverse mix of humanity, I met the reality of plurality head-on. I delighted in a deep-felt kinship with the countless strangers into whose lives I had a small glimpse. This gave me a taste of the unity of human experience amidst such extremes of cultural expression. The witness of our common humanity, built upon so many varieties of human struggle and aspiration, enchanted my youthful imagination.

With this exposure, a flood of questions of meaning washed over me, and gave birth to a new sense of self: more connected, more curious, more conscious. It became clear to me that my life belonged to a bigger story – indeed, my travels had introduced me to a much more vast field of possibilities. No doubt, there was a part for me, as for each of us, to play in bringing greater consciousness and compassion into a world darkened with sorrow. However, I was still much at a loss to know where I fit. Years later, I had the wonderful opportunity to spend two six-month sojourns in the Eastern Himalayas engaged in community development projects.

On our shrinking planet, the dynamics of an emerging global village present a complex reality of relationship, more challenging than ever-before imagined. With ever-intensifying population pressures, we are becoming acutely aware of the total interdependence of all phenomena. Earth, air, fire, water and human life are woven into an intricate web of relationships that form an integrated bio-spiritual whole – where matter and meaning merge, and whose fundamental order finds its basis in the law of love.

Within human interactions, the intentions and deeds of each individual have a far-reaching impact on the whole global community, for better or worse. Truly, everyone has a responsibility, not only for personal well-being, but also for the happiness of all beings. The formidable task of cultivating a depth of friendship that reaches out inclusively to the totality of humankind constitutes the challenge of our times.

Certainly, in the face of widespread human suffering, our true hope for happiness lies in the goal of universal love – everyone's survival hinges on our ability to move to a higher viewpoint, beyond ego and ethnocentricity. Such a transformative leap requires nobler intention and strengthened ethical integrity in order to expose the monopoly of wealth, media control, moral evil, and gross injustice that comprise the dark dynamics of social decline. Global peace can only be built on the basis of a more just world.

We have entered an age of mass communication, and consciousness is on a steep expansion curve that is generating a radical new vision of reality. With deepened sensitivity to our universal yearning for interconnection, human beings everywhere are receiving the summons to transcend short-sighted self-interest and collaborate in the task of forging a new global reality. The keen determination to go on advancing the goal of human solidarity is motivated by a desire to affirm and celebrate our differences, and join them together into an experience of universal harmony.

For the whole depends on each part, and each part on the whole. We find our true belonging inside widening networks of friendship where we escape meaninglessness and isolation. The contribution to the whole asked of each individual lies in accord with one's personal calling and creative capabilities. As we bring new patterns of relationship into being, the quality of our cross-cultural interactions is enriched, leading to an increase of global happiness.

differentiation and unity

On the personal level, authenticity asks us simply to be true to ourselves – and thus calls us to a committed journey of progressive self-discovery. Self-actualization requires deep interiority, a quality of self-presence, wise insight, keen discernment, and steady self-determination. Through the awakening of original creativity, we find our place and fulfil our purpose under the sun.

In fact, personal development forms the basis for all social integration – one's difference is essential to the well-being of everyone. It is not about going it alone: when we lose ourselves in the unreality of the separate self, believing that we exist apart from the whole, we become disconnected from our source of vital meaning. In truth, individual achievements of growth, when joined with the accomplishments of others, create a powerful force for collective transformation. We thrive inside groups.

A cultural heritage provides a matrix of belonging for its people - each clan, tribe, or ethnic group endeavours to nurture its own well-being, and to preserve and protect its own unique identity. In this age of plurality, we are now exposed to a myriad of values and meanings derived from a wide variety of mythic origins. We are being drawn into a new depth of cross-cultural encounter; called from isolation to interrelatedness, and from self-sufficiency to interdependence. Indeed, our diverse cultural vocations are being woven into larger webs of human interaction that seem ever more complex with the march of time.

In the interplay of vast differences, we are challenged to seek out the truth of love that will guide us towards that genuine happiness longed for by everyone under the sun. As we tap into deeper wisdom, and develop a new sensitivity and appreciation of *otherness*, we will find a stronger will to justice and peace. New depths of interpersonal and intercultural trust will enable us to traverse new thresholds of consciousness; and through the dynamic integration of our differences, to discover our essential unity.

celebration of diversity

Letting things be different opens the door to diversity. As biodiversity provides the basis for the resilience of an ecosystem, likewise, within the human sphere, the building blocks for unity are found in the treasure chest of our vast differences. When tensions of difference are held creatively, the friction engendered by personal and cultural diversity fires a desire and drive for wider wisdom, deeper truth, richer meaning.

No one person or group or culture can claim to have all the right answers – nor all the right questions for that matter. Every perspective enlarges our grasp of understanding. And so diversity calls forth dialogue, where each impassioned version of truth exists as a counterpoint for other viewpoints in a creative process of transformation.

The miracle of dialogue builds from finesse in communication – deep listening, honest self-expression, mutual respect, openness to otherness. Genuine dialogue includes a back-and-forth exchange of points of view and counterpoints, attentiveness to verifiable data, feedback loops, critical thinking, wise discernment, and sensitive understanding. Through in-depth encounter and exchange, we weave ever-larger tapestries of truth.

As we join our differences and seek out a larger wisdom of life, it helps to make a clear distinction between uniformity and universality. Our efforts to safeguard individual dignity and strengthen cultural identity are in no way an attempt to make everyone the same. For indeed, the unique gifts found in each person and culture beg full affirmation and expression.

But, at the same time, there are universal values that ought never to be compromised – human rights that protect the powerless from persecution, exploitation, and discrimination; as well as those human rights that promote access to education and health, freedom of expression, and the dignity of self-determination.

At the heart of human longing is the universal hope for a love that will bind us as *one*. We long for a solidarity that weaves together human solitude, and thrives in the appreciation of the extraordinary riches found within each culture. The world, once thought to be a big *melting pot* of differences, is now better described as a *mosaic*: differences woven together, accentuating one another, but not melted down. No one culture can ever be replaced by another, for each contributes uniquely to the ongoing evolution of the story of our universe.

Modern day satellite images show us the breadth of immense weather systems, i.e. tropical storms and hurricanes that span oceans and continents, and that reveal a larger set of dynamics at play in the Earth's atmosphere beyond the local inflections of weather. I stand in awe of these stunning overviews from outer space – they present to my spiritual imagination an image of a unified field of friendship binding all humanity in a bond of loving kindness.

What a gift to have met Jihad – our friendship embodies the hope of the ages for unity within the human family based upon healthy interdependence. Our conversation ended as it began as Jihad further expounded on the true meaning of his name: "*False jihad* has no foundation. The test of truth is what brings lasting peace and fulfillment to us; what is genuine, real, and truly beautiful."

"*True jihad* is when I dedicate myself to the widest circle of care possible, with myself as the centre of giving and the furthest stranger as the radius. I try to keep my radius as far and deep as I can. Wisdom is nothing other than seeing yourself in others, and understanding that each person's story is really part of your own."

"Every time I see or touch the humanity of another, I experience an intensity of feeling. Love is the steady adrenaline that drives me, gives me courage and a sense of purpose – it is self-generating. Life becomes a real nightmare when love is absent."

14. Peace Consciousness

*Many people think excitement is happiness...
But when you are excited you are not peaceful.
True happiness is based on peace.*
Thich Nhat Hanh

*The lover of justice is possessed by justice
and inherits its strength.*
Meister Eckhart

*Someday, after mastering the winds, the waves, the tides and
gravity, we shall harness for God the energies of love,
and then, for a second time in the history of the world,
man will have discovered fire.*
Teilhard de Chardin

cultivating simplicity

The word *rhizome* came up in a conversation I was having with Mark about what was motivating him to keep his life simple. "I like the word a lot," he said. "For me, it is a symbol of an unseen energy that's animating the purpose of our lives. We are not conscious of this hidden purpose, nor can we manipulate it, but by simplifying our lives we can become open to this underlying current that connects us with meaning."

Rhizome, by definition, is an underground root system – subterranean stems that grow horizontally and send shoots above the surface.

Mark Smith

Mark suggested that *rhizome* represents a below-surface self where his life unfolds as an invisible process, as opposed to the different ways in which one's life finds expression above surface. It is the *rhizome of meaning* that endures while the outer manifestations of self appear and disappear.

"More and more, I have discovered that the real zen of life is just being. Simplicity really comes down to self-presence. Simplicity is not an end in itself. Its ultimate purpose is to open us to experiences that are meaningful by allowing us to pay attention to what has enduring value – the rhizome of our lives. If we can simplify our lives enough, we can move beyond our consumption of experiences and get in touch with empathy and compassion."

I asked Mark what he meant by the *consumption of experiences*, and he responded: "There seems to be a sort of symbiotic relationship between the way life is marketed to us and our addiction to experience. When I was younger, I travelled all over the place, and wanted to have as many experiences as I could. I was trying to validate who I was by consuming experiences. I know that my travels had value and purpose, but reflecting back I can see that I was never really very present to what I was experiencing. It was as though the idea of the experiences had more value than the experience itself."

Mark further elaborated: "I spent a lot of money, effort, and time medicating myself to process the discomfort I felt from not being at home in my body or in my inner world of raw emotions. Running from my inner loneliness I constantly tried to connect with others, and went out of my way to have interesting experiences at the expense of stillness and solitude. I thought that my life wasn't worth anything unless it was validated from the outside. I was afraid of not being able to realize all of my ambitions, not being able to have continuous adrenaline rushes. Though I was having a little bit of fun, to be honest there wasn't much love manifesting in my life."

Mark further elaborated on his struggle to live simply in a complex world. "Complexity is marketed through mass media, presenting ideas and images of what our lives are supposed to be. It is geared towards ambition, and trying to make our lives overly comfortable and secure. Complexity distracts you from the reality of your life, whereas simplicity reveals your true path. Simplicity is now one of the sounding boards I use to make important decisions in my life. My motivation is built on wanting to keep my life as grounded and authentic as possible. When making choices about my day-to-day living, the key question is: does the choice foster simplicity or does it complicate things?"

"Rhizome is synonymous with one's inner resonance, being open to the purpose of life experienced in the body and the mind. It has to do with the energy we bring into the body through food and movement: aliveness for me comes from eating well, doing yoga, practicing shiatsu, running, lifting weights, walking, and cycling. It also has to do with meditative practices: healing the mind, staying calm, cultivating greater awareness, connecting to others through compassion. I often think that we are afraid of the creative capacity we would have if our minds and bodies were in full form. The real challenge is to face that fear and allow ourselves to become our healthiest possibility."

When Mark was 20 years old, his feet landed in Taizé – a monastery in southern France where young people came from all over the world to have an experience of monastic life. The allurement for Mark in going to Taizé was "…to unplug from the momentum of my life. I had been teaching in Poland, meeting all kinds of people, climbing mountains, visiting museums, and consuming experiences."

"Something in the world of monastic values resonated inside me, pointing me in the direction of simplicity and stability. I wanted to remove myself from all the cultural stimuli that were telling me that life happens outside myself, and filling me with fear and doubt. I needed more inwardness."

"Taizé was where I came back to myself. I was forced to unplug – there were three periods of silence a day. It was the first time I experienced the rhizome of my life: by stopping my life and calming my body, my mind had space to rest and I felt the overwhelming presence of life. Thinking, controlling, and rationalizing all melted away. It was kind of like untying of all the mental blocks I had created in my life, in my relationships, in my habit behaviours. I was learning to let go of everything that wasn't me."

"It was in this experience of nothingness that I came in contact with something overflowing in myself. Getting in touch with one's authentic self in the everyday world is challenging – it takes mindfulness, lots of practice, and a little bit of grace."

hidden power

The *rhizome* conversation with Mark sparked reflection upon the escalating violence in our world, and the question of how we are to find genuine peace – not only personal harmony, but also interpersonal and ecological accord.

Why does peace, which is at the heart of human yearning, remain so exhaustingly elusive? Why do our age-old questions about human conflict and cruelty go without answers? What is lacking in our consciousness and intentionality that prevent us from building a world where everyone belongs?

These questions led me to ponder how best to activate the *rhizome* energies of love that comprise who we really are. These energies, which are intrinsic to our nature, need to be cultivated in order to find full expression in our lives, and patiently wait for the light of day. My further deliberation found a focus on two essential seeds of non-violence: the force of humility and the power of forgiveness.

I have always felt an extraordinary pressure when trying to *make myself into a somebody*. One way I attempt to let off a build-up of this kind of tension is to give myself permission to be a *nobody*. Though appearing to be an act of self-negation, it reflects my effort to stop trying to be someone I am not, and to become the person I really want to be. Or, as it is commonly said, to *get more real*.

Humility is often seen as weakness, but only from the vantage point of the complex ego. Authentic humility, in fact, allows one's heart to open and constitutes an individual's true strength. Vanity is humility's opposite – it takes us into a world of striving and breeds endless complexity. A vain person puts a lot of effort into looking good and getting ahead of others, but there is deep emptiness when the song-and-dance of the ego exhausts itself.

As we come to discover that there is no one to impress, we are freed from having to make a show of our achievements. When our need for recognition is met in a healthy way, the inner violence of artificial self-importance falls away. Living from a depth of authenticity, a humble person embraces both limitation and potential, and thereby is able to focus on *true possibility*. It is the way of humility that reveals what makes us truly special.

Adding to what has been said, humility is ultimately about self-respect and introduces us to the wisdom of self-emptying. This has nothing to do with humiliation and shaming, or putting oneself down. Self-emptying is the downsizing of the ego – whereby we do not negate self-esteem, but rather learn to trust our intrinsic goodness. The humble person pursues a power of virtue which is grounded in the knowledge that one is not the source of attained virtue, but rather its vehicle.

In the same root system as humility, forgiveness germinates from an underground rhizome of peace. As we empty ourselves of attachments to perfection demanded by the false self, we critique our own moral performance; and, by admitting our mistakes, we are able to identify with others in their imperfection. This activates a power of humility that inspires acts of forgiveness, and in turn strengthens personal integrity.

By choosing to forgive our mistakes, we learn to focus on a gentle correction of self. As we pardon self, we open ourselves to a larger freedom of love that pardons those who have offended us. To forgive is to unfreeze the past – to find a way out of hurt and hate, to go beyond resentment and revenge. In place of trying to get even, we can choose a way of non-violence that steps outside the repetitious cycle of vengeance.

Non-violence is not about non-action, or surrender to injustice. Certainly, we cannot have peace without justice. Authentic relationship is guided by justice. To act justly is to become attuned to the suffering we inflict on ourselves and on one another, and to investigate the causes. This requires thorough honesty – it forces us to confront self-deception and our own personal failures to love truthfully.

The call to authenticity invites our participation in justice-making. It is a journey of love that pulls us away from a narrow world of trivial self-satisfactions. In the growing unrest of our times, the dynamics of social decline are made evident by global depression, widespread inequality, terrorism and corruption, the concentration of wealth and power, human desperation, and ecological degradation. Injustice manifests in so many different ways: extreme luxury, obsessive consumption, untold waste, the exploitation of natural resources, industrial pollution, the ideology of materialism, the thrust towards greater production and militarism. Injustice is also revealed by the fact that the poor have no access to natural capital.

The ongoing evolution of consciousness indicates that true peace will only be found by stepping outside violence completely. Unquestionably, history attests to the fact that violence always begets more violence – this points to our need to relinquish economic inequality, vengeance, scapegoating, hate, discrimination, and even the notion of a just war. The truth of love gives peace its strongest leverage. Love releases us from the prison of violence that has robbed us of our true destiny – it is love that discloses where genuine happiness is to be found.

task of consciousness

Even as our technological powers have taken giant steps forward, our intention to love lags, and often completely falters. Why is compassion lacking? What puts us so much at odds with human kindness?

Why do we refuse to offer our happiness to one another?

The chaos and complexity of our times call forth a new quality of consciousness, and spur our intention to learn a larger love. Beyond the conquest of external environments, a new emphasis needs to be placed on a mastery of the inner self. No longer can the pursuit of comfort and material prosperity be the all-important focus, for our true hope rests upon an inner training that fosters happiness for all beings.

If we act solely on the basis of individual or cultural self-interest, violent rivalry will only escalate, and we will slowly destroy ourselves and one another. Human greed and cruelty are as cancerous cells of a body at war inside itself. The parallel is clear: ruthless self-interest assigns us a place on death row.

Planet Earth now faces grave challenges: food-water-air crises, ecological disequilibrium, war and brutality, and widespread poverty. This bring humankind to a huge turning point – to tap into our collective human potential, the global community urgently needs a critical path of inspired intention, enlarged consciousness, and determined action.

The task of peace demands a breakthrough into love, with a focus on learning to live from an open heart. For love reveals values and inspires truth. It lets us see the good of the whole, the web of life in its entirety. Only a committed intention of love will open possibilities of peace not yet imagined.

A cornerstone of authenticity is the development of a science of consciousness that awakens a compassionate sensitivity to human suffering, and expands our capacity to care for others and oneself. Each of us is asked to embrace an ethos of radical love.

Beyond moral or political domination, beyond intolerance, beyond rivalry and greed, lies a true peace. That peace will be realized as we develop a profound respect for everyone. Though mostly strangers to one another, we the co-habitants on this sacred planet are invited into a dance of sacred friendship.

As Mark spoke about the intention of simplicity that is guiding him on his life journey, he brought forth several compelling images to describe the *rhizome of peace*: beauty, non-accumulation, stillness, non-distraction. At one point in our conversation, Mark talked about the aliveness he experiences when camping with his family: "...the ultimate in simplicity: the magic moment on a canoe trip when you pack everything you need into one small canoe – your food, clothing, gear, and relationship. It is a great teaching in living the art of simplicity."

"If we can simplify our lives enough, we can move beyond our consumption of experiences and get in touch with empathy and compassion."

15. Authentic Bliss

My life is my message.
Mahatma Gandhi

*Place yourself in the middle of the stream of power and
wisdom which flows into you as life,
place yourself in the full center of that flood,
then you are without effort impelled to truth,
to right, and a perfect contentment.*
Ralph Waldo Emerson

*Find a place where there is joy,
and the joy will burn out the pain.*
Joseph Campbell

becoming who I am

Bhaskar began having back spasms in his early 20s. By his account, his muscle contractions came from competitive tennis and from work-related heavy lifting. "My back kept locking up, I was in a constant state of fear not knowing when it would tighten up next, how intense it would be, and for how long. I was very fortunate at the time to meet a great yoga master. I remember that moment like it happened yesterday. This man had a quality of absolute fearlessness. I thought if I could be just a little bit like him, yoga would be a worthwhile practice. He took me in like an apprentice-son, and that is how my yoga journey began."

This encounter marked a pivotal turning point in Bhaskar's life. He grew up in India, then worked as an engineer in the Middle East, and by the time Bhaskar made Canada his home at the age of 25, the practice of yoga had become his driving passion.

Bhaskar Goswami

"I was an engineer by day and a yoga teacher by night. I was on a path towards optimal health. I began to feel really awake and alive – developing a very calm and sharp mind, and a steady and healthy body. I wanted so much to share this beautiful growth experience with my co-workers, some of whom were struggling."

"Though I entered into yoga practice because of my back pain, the engineer in me was very surprised to discover that yoga is a precise science of self-awareness – it was therefore very appealing to my *engineering* mind. It seemed to me that there was such a strong correlation between yoga and engineering. Both follow the exact same process: investigating how something functions, how it can be used, how it can be made better. Yoga applies these same questions to one's body-mind structure. This knowledge brings miraculous insights."

Bhaskar continued to extol the merits of yoga: "Integrity can be seen as the union that yoga speaks to. Integrity is wholeness. By addressing the fundamental question of *who I am* the practice brought me, sometimes willingly and sometimes kicking and screaming, into self-awareness. The yoga sutras offer step-by-step instructions that teach you how to calm the mind, and awaken the truth of who you are. Authenticity is based on inner awareness. You've got to go inside yourself. There you discover qualities such as compassion, loving kindness, generosity, acceptance, and fearlessness that are all attributes of integrity, co-existing and containing each other. They are all reflections of the same light – the light of consciousness."

I asked Bhaskar to comment on that which robs us of our authenticity. "Personal integrity is based on being truthful to yourself in each moment. There have certainly been times when I have played the game of inauthenticity. Being blindsided, I made choices that violated my true nature, choices that just felt wrong. The loss of integrity, for me, can always be traced back to a fear of some sort – perhaps a fear of not having enough, of not being appreciated, or fears related to self-esteem issues."

"By loosening your grip on false identity, you are able to unmask any illusions of being in control." Bhaskar wanted to put an emphasis on how authenticity is tied into the discovery of one's innermost self: "As you get unstuck from any one way of perceiving yourself, you begin to move towards who you truly are. When you identify with your thoughts, emotions, sensory inputs, wants, expectations, or with anything in the external world of changing phenomena, you sow seeds of inauthenticity based on mistaken identity. Your authenticity is found as you come into contact with your changeless self."

Bhaskar knows this first-hand – after 20 years as a yoga practitioner, he was struck with an extremely rare and life-threatening disease (Guillain-Barre Syndrome) that left his body completely paralyzed. "My body went from being fully functional to being totally debilitated within a span of two weeks. It took about five months of intense treatment and physical rehabilitation to return to a functioning state."

As he stared into the razor's edge of life, Bhaskar tells of coming into deeper contact with his changeless self. "There were bleak moments of helpless pain. There were also beautiful moments when I had the privilege of teaching yoga to fellow patients at the rehabilitation center even though I myself could barely move. Through it all, there was, and still is, a tangible and undeniable presence of what I can best describe as an undercurrent of perfection behind the entire experience. This must be the energy that moves through the universe that so many great teachers point to. Now, whether bleak or beautiful, I am that much more keenly aware of its presence. It has a way of removing the drama and igniting a sense of awe for all that is."

I invited him to say more about what he meant when he spoke of an *undercurrent of perfection*. "It's that innate feeling of knowing that it had to be that way. It is a total acceptance of how the story is unfolding, no matter how much the joy or suffering. It comes from acknowledging the reality of the present moment, exactly as it is."

epic adventure

We are a part of the energy that moves the universe – an energy that invites each of us to discover the truth of love that lies at the heart of all reality. The true hero path marks out the challenge we each face to become who we are. That path, described in the wisdom traditions of all ages, brings us into an experience of full human aliveness.

Authenticity issues the call to each of us to set forth on an adventure of self-discovery. We feel incomplete, and seek completion; we feel fragmented, and long for wholeness; we feel disconnected, and need to belong. And so we strain forward in search of a larger love, not yet known. In our longing for *oneness*, separate identity begins to dissolve giving us a taste of the bliss of the boundless love that is our deep desire.

As we become more keenly aware of the interconnectedness of all life, our sense of personal purpose links us to a universal truth of meaning. Through rendering our lives to the common good versus the private self, a new vision of reality emerges that takes us beyond the deception of base egotism into an expanded freedom of love.

All of us are players in the dynamic story of our developing global village in which a new world-wide culture of wisdom wants to emerge. We no longer can live by the rule of survival-of-the-fittest. As a new ethos of peace and compassion breaks into minds and hearts across the planet, progressive consciousness urges us towards radical co-operation.

Personal authenticity is the starting point for social transformation. Our commitment to self-development, guided by the steady discernment of what it means to live a genuine life, brings us into networks of interaction that support mutual learning, growth, and transformation. A network continuously re-makes itself – each player participates in the transformation of other players in the network.

No longer do we speak of hierarchies, but rather webs of interactive life – patterns of purposeful relationships within an integrated whole. In the emerging global community, we are discovering our lives to be inseparable – no one exists in isolation. This invites us to learn a more advanced language of love. As our capacity for compassion is enlarged, the needs of others become less invisible and beg more loving kindness.

visionary fire

We all sense the extraordinary future that is waiting to be born. In order to tap into our potential for endless creativity, it is necessary to activate new spiritual imagination to guide us through some difficult stages of growth. To evoke that future, we must turn our attention inwards in order to become sensitive to those symbolic images sourced from deep within ourselves that will lead us forward along the path of our becoming.

Perhaps this inner process starts in the remembrance of those images which first ignited the dream of one's life, and that continue to push us in the direction of authenticity. From becoming to becoming, we are guided by visions that keep us attuned to the stories that our lives wish to write – the task of shaping personal intention requires a continuous refinement of values and meanings. Often a close friend or wise mentor is instrumental in helping to dig up questions of purpose that most want attention.

Added to what has been said, one's power of self-determination finds its basis in a fire of vision that motivates continuous self-discovery – a steady practice of awareness enables discernment and deeds to walk hand-in-hand. Some individuals are task-oriented, though not supported by a guiding vision. Others are visionary, but never come down to earth – they lack the ability to translate intention into determined action.

To be truly alive with growth is discover one's infinite possibilities within the interplay of matter and mind and meaning within our lives. Challenge is found at every level of being: we care for our bodies through developed habits of nutrition, exercise, sleep; we attend to our psyches through habits of mindfulness and emotional literacy; foremost, we commit ourselves to the long learning that teaches our hearts to love. We take time to be with ourselves, time to study, time to heal, and time to play.

It is always a great blessing to find a small group of kindred spirits with whom to share visionary fire. Friends who empower one another in self-realization are truly alive in the delight of mutual presence one to the other. And it is within the context of committed friendship that we learn our biggest lessons in generosity and gratitude. Our passion for authenticity is deeply enlivened through reciprocated support and encouragement, enabling us to actualize our individual and collective potential more fully.

promise of bliss

To be authentic is to be alert, intelligent, clear, decisive, relaxed, compassionate – it is to be in love. The commitment to know and be true to self opens us to the dance of life. To be fully alive is to experience the delight of ongoing self-development and the vibrant energy of unconditional love. As we engage self, the other, and the cosmos more deeply, we come in touch with the universal law of harmony and the promise of bliss that it reveals – in this way, we come to know the meaning of genuine happiness.

Equanimity is realized through learning to *resist nothing*. It is found in the experience of deep acceptance – in the joyful embrace of life as it arises in each moment. By being keenly sensitive to beauty and suffering, we are able to draw forth our capacity for a new potential of creativity and compassion.

Bliss becomes real as we write the lyrics of our own song of authenticity, and slowly learn to sound the right notes. Best known for his dictum to *follow your bliss*, Joseph Campbell suggests that when we are on our bliss track, new doors will always open and that we will encounter people who are in our field of bliss. We are on the right track when the life we ought to be living is the one we are living.

However, attachment to an ego track will cost us our authenticity – and, in turn, our bliss. Fatal attraction is the hallmark of ego-striving that draws us towards pleasure and profit, fame and fortune. If we walk down the dead-end paths of fear and greed and ignorance, we sow seeds of future suffering.

Certainly, gratitude is the high road of bliss – it gives evidence of one's evolution from grasping to giving. The low road is marked by both the fear of scarcity and the compulsion to acquire, that surely lead to rivalry. Moreover, beliefs of entitlement walk the low road and fuel much resentment. However, in the experience of gratitude, beyond envy and greed, our focus turns more to what we have received than what we do not have. In this way, we tap into a consciousness of abundance. The law of sharing addresses lack and limitation by introducing us to a confidence that there is enough of everything for everyone. In fact, goods are not used up – they multiply as we share them.

Our journey to wholeness always asks us to address the different sources of disintegration found within ourselves, and to befriend both the mud of our imperfection and the law of our impermanence. In this way, we foster an integrity of insight and action that leads to a progressive flowering of awareness and strengthening of intention – in turn, that lets us taste the joy of coming home to ourselves and others.

Now, on the other side of his muddy ordeal, Bhaskar is back playing tennis. I asked how his game was going, and this was his answer: "The integrity of my performance is built on five S's: strength, stamina, speed, skill, and suppleness." I came in from another angle: "Are you winning your matches?" Bhaskar was quick to rebound: "When you are not losing energy by identifying with the hero or the zero, you are far more focused and effective. Win or lose, the witness of your performance is the real game-changer."

Each threshold of change in our lives sets before us the daunting challenge to heed the call to authenticity. The promise of bliss is realized through the living of an open life that reaches for ever higher levels of body-mind-spirit integration. There is no end to self-discovery, and therefore, no limit on happiness. Ultimately, our freedom is experienced through leaps into higher consciousness that teach the heart to open. May we all grow in the wisdom of authenticity that ignites and sustains the fire of love.

"When you identify with your thoughts, emotions, sensory inputs, wants, expectations, or with anything in the external world of changing phenomena, you sow seeds of inauthenticity based on mistaken identity."

Acknowledgments

Thanking everyone who has supported me in bringing forth this book is an impossible task – simply because there are too many of you to thank.

Of course, the superstars are those 15 friends whose paraphrased reflections create the back bone of this book. I have learned much along the way, and indeed, have had an amazing amount of fun. No doubt, the encouragement towards authenticity that we have bestowed on one another is the precious gift that all of us have shared. Thank you Scott, Christelle, Eli, Fabien, Lucas, Heather, Mike, Jen, Barkley, Pete, Leyla, Solomon, Jihad, Mark, and Bhaskar – each of you lives inside my heart!

A good book needs good editors. I have been very lucky to have Nicholas Bilof and Mark Smith sift through the 36,000 words within these pages, and make sure that every word found just the right place. Thanks for your labour of authenticity.

I would like to single out three other key players who have made an outstanding contribution: Dan Juras, whose boundless enthusiasm and skills as a photographer are mirrored in these pages; Larry

Cassini, who has walked with the project every step of the way, and who, with his daughter Emilie, has composed the beautiful music title *Song of Authenticity* to accompany this book (listen to the music on the website, and inside the future e-book version); and Natalie Riviere, whose vibrant energy and expertise have shaped the strategies for getting-this-book-out-there.

I am also grateful to Christelle Francois and Helen Downie whose wonderful enthusiasm has found expression in the organization of our book launch. I too owe a great debt of gratitude to Joan Carmichael who has been my computer guru, and made my writing tasks so much easier.

There is more to follow: an e-publication will be forthcoming within the next few months, and will include video links inside the book. A big thank you to Jean-Marc Duchesne who trekked around with a camera for eight months to capture the images and record the voices of the authenticity cast.

My gratitude goes out to four persons whose generous financial contributions and wonderful encouragement have made this publication possible: Clare Hallward, Catherine McKenty, Patricia Lemieux, and the late Audrey Brune.

Last not least, my heartfelt thanks to Drew MacEachern for the cover design, and Carole Zabbal-Wynne for the book layout design. You have been outstanding team players!

ABOUT THE AUTHOR

Author Stephen Sims is the founding director of the IASIS Foundation - an awareness education project that has, since the early 80s, developed a far-reaching dialogue on themes related to the wisdom of personal transformation. The work of this foundation seeks to empower self-discovery, encourage the enlargement of consciousness and compassion, and foster physical wellness, emotional literacy, and spiritual potential. Over a span of more than three decades, Steve has led vision quests, support groups and small interactive learning circles to stimulate self-enquiry and authenticity. Wilderness adventure outings have been an integral part of the IASIS project - Steve himself is an ardent canoe enthusiast.

After graduating from university in the late 60s, Steve taught in schools both in Canada and Australia, and travelled extensively through Asia. In the early 70s, he worked as a paramedic with the sick and destitute dying at Jesu Ashram in the Darjeeling region of northern India. Returning to his native Montreal, Steve assumed the role of a lay chaplain at Concordia University. This preceded his appointment as program director of the Spera Foundation, a drug rehabilitation centre – his work in addiction led to the establishment of the IASIS dialogues. At a later stage, he served as director of a hospitality house for the homeless.

In the mid-90s, Steve went back to India where he initiated similar dialogues with educators and community development workers throughout the Eastern Himalayas. This cross-cultural experience was the catalyst for his first writing project, as well as for the establishment of the Padua Dialogue – an interdisciplinary wisdom forum exploring the healing arts, the transformational sciences, and the teachings of different spiritual traditions. His other community involvements have included youth outreach, prison support groups, visitation to the elderly, and palliative care for the terminally ill.

The Wisdom of Authenticity, Steve's second book, gives us a glimpse into the interactive dialogue circles that he has been facilitating over the last 33 years. *River of Awareness*, his first book, was published in 2009 with a variety of thematic reflections that make reference to his wide range of life experience.

The author can be contacted at:
steve@stephenksims.com

www.ingramcontent.com/pod-product-compliance
Lightning Source LLC
Chambersburg PA
CBHW071214090426
42736CB00014B/2820